CW00590392

Edited by Chris Charlesworth
Cover & Book designed by Alun Evans, 4i Limited
Picture research by David Brolan

ISBN: 0.7119.3492.4
Order No: OP47326

Exclusive Distributors
Book Sales Limited,
8/9 Frith Street,
London W1V 5TZ, UK.

Music Sales Corporation,
225 Park Avenue South,
New York, NY 10003, USA.

Music Sales Pty Limited,
120 Rothschild Avenue,
Rosebery, NSW 2018, Australia.

To the Music Trade only:
Music Sales Limited,
8/9, Frith Street,
London W1V 5TZ, UK.

Photo credits:
David Anderson/SIN: back cover bottom left; Matt
Anker/Retna: 61; Jay Blakesberg/Retna: 55;
George Chin: 57, 64, 70; Jeffrey Davy/Retna: 40;
Jeffrey Davy/SIN: 17; Steve Double/Retna: 19, 23,
36, 43t; Martyn Goodacre/SIN: front cover, back
cover top left, 2/3, 10, 13, 14, 43b; Steve
Gullick/Retna: 49; Jane Huntington/SIN: 76/77;
Neils Van Iperen/Retna: 22, 68/69, 72, 84, 85, 96;
Sandra Johnson/Retna: 62; Don Lewis/SIN: 38/39,
79; London Features International: back cover
bottom right, 8, 9, 12, 16, 20, 21, 28/29, 32/33, 37,
67, 87; Jeffrey Mayer/Star File: 6; Tony Mott/SIN:
44; Phil Nicholls/SIN: 48; Chuck Pulin/Star File: 47;
Steve Pyke/Retna: 27; Relay Photos: 50, 51; Ed
Sirrs/Retna: 24, 25, 30/31, 41, 52, 53, 56, 81, 82;
Paul Stanley/SIN: 1; Stephen Sweet/Retna: 89; Ian
Tilton/Retna: 34, 58, 75.

Every effort has been made to trace the copyright
holders of the photographs in this book but one or
two were unreachable. We would be grateful if the
photographers concerned would contact us.

Printed and bound in Singapore.

A catalogue record for this book is available from
the British Library.

Thanks to Gillian Gaar.

nirvana

Officially, 1991 was the year Punk broke. Overturning years of corporate oppression, the underground clawed its way to the surface, and slid into the secret treasure houses of the establishment. One by one, the bastions fell: major label chequebooks, college radio, MTV, the Top 40 stations, *Time, Vanity Fair, Vogue*. The same irresistible wave that swept commentators, talent scouts and other big-league leeches to Seattle also washed through Hollywood, London, New York. Hell, they even made a video about it - complete with parental advisory sticker to prove that the revolution still had sharp teeth.

Strangely enough, the revolution was documented by Geffen Home Video, a subsidiary of the David Geffen Company - part of the multi-media empire of a man who, twenty years ago, brought another rock revolution into the streets, when he corralled a generation of sensitive singer-songwriters and turned them into even more sensitive millionaires. And the revolution was soon being measured in statistics, with dollar signs at the start of every number - $250,000 advances, $40,000,000 in record sales, umpteen billion staked on the future of rock'n'roll.

For some of the revolutionaries, that was no revolution at all. To the hard core of the American punk underground, the battle was everything: the mere fact that you were cornered in a bunker, the last gang in town, picking off stragglers with a misfiring .45 - all that was more important than victory. There couldn't be victory, in fact, without compromise. And so for the punk fanzines, 1991 had a sickly smell. It was the year Punk sold out.

Between the two lines of barricades - one claiming victory over the infantile hordes of corporate rock, the other carping that the oppressed had become the oppressors - even the definitions had begun to dissolve. What kind of Punk was this that sounded like warmed-over Black Sabbath, that depended on The Beatles for its hooks and Led Zeppelin for its dynamics? Where was the border between punk and metal - and between revivalism and progress? Was teen spirit a rallying call, a cynical marketing manoeuvre or an adolescent deodorant? Who was screwing who?

Even the battleground was tilting. The word in 1991 was Seattle - just as it had been in 1989, 6,000 miles away in the hype-hungry rock media of London. Cultural pundits assembled in the city which has been consistently voted the most liveable in America, and stripped it bare in the search for significance. Crossing the mountains from the East to reach the Western strip of the USA, which is isolated from the great mass of the continent by peaks and deserts, it was easy to grasp at frontier metaphors - to find in Seattle the last outpost of pre-civilisation, a more innocent, primeval society excluded from the cultural breezes that had fuelled the rest of the nation.

Even this cliché disintegrated under the murkiest of glances. Far from being a backwoods holdout against the Twentieth Century, Seattle turned out to be an oasis of Art and Decency - with a flourishing gay scene, theatres, ballet, opera, parks, plenty of slack for the outdoor life. Narrow the focus to rock'n'roll, and the city was still no hillbilly hangover from the time when Bing Crosby was Washington State's prime cultural export. From Seattle and its overspill towns had come Jimi Hendrix, Robert Cray, Quincy Jones, The Sonics, Paul Revere and The Raiders, and one of the hottest metal bands of the Eighties, Queensryche. And one thing I forgot to mention: Nirvana don't even come from Seattle.

The British rock press hyped Mudhoney and Tad, the American underground backed Sonic Youth and The Butthole Surfers, the Seattle media tipped The Dan Reed Network and Soundgarden. Until 'Nevermind' was released in the autumn of 1991, Nirvana's traditional place was at the end of a sentence - as in "other bands on Sub Pop include The Walkabouts, Swallow and Nirvana". Neither the first of the 'alternative' Washington State bands to be nominated for a Grammy (Soundgarden) nor to win a gold record (Alice In Chains), Nirvana didn't so much come from behind as from outside. They were immigrants in Seattle, late arrivals at Sub Pop, afterthoughts in the first great assault on Europe - and they cleaned up, sliding to success along the paths swept bare by Sonic Youth and Mudhoney.

Sell-outs or sneak thieves, Nirvana have paid a price for their platinum albums. Maybe they were in training for the major labels from the start, but by indie terms, where productivity equals authenticity, they've been as slothful as the sludge-rock bands who first inspired them to trash a guitar. One album written by 1988, issued in 1989; another effectively written by 1990; and then close to three years of artistic emasculation, as the band - and particularly leader, songwriter and reluctant superhero Kurt Cobain - floundered in the choppy waters of international fame, reaching out for crutches that often as not were built from barbed wire, riding the downhill train to excess and maybe to disintegration.

Since 'Nevermind' hit the charts, Nirvana's career has had nothing to do with music - or with creating anything other than dollars and havoc. They've fallen victim to the built-in claws of the world-wide record industry, which are there to squeeze the udders of the sacred cow until it bleeds. And if it bleeds to death, no matter: there's always another cow waiting for sainthood. For Nirvana, the struggle in 1993 is survival.

The searchlight focus on the private life of Cobain, his wife Courtney Love and their baby, Frances Bean, has left the family in the position of convicted felons, desperate for an appeal hearing in a higher court. The tiny details that make up everyday life have become cultural totems: did the Cobains knowingly risk their unborn child with the poison of heroin? Is Courtney Love a bleached-blonde milkmaid, feeding off that undernourished cow? Ask magazines like *Vanity Fair* - or the *Globe*, who upped the ante in the Cobain vs. Heroin contest by painting the outlines of a possible child abuse case. Cobain and Love reacted to aggression with irony, but soon discovered that irony means nothing to those without imagination. Flailing wildly at those they saw as their tormentors, closing the door to their friends, Kurt and Courtney have become embattled holdouts against the media hordes. Millions of people who have never listened to their music now know their names and have already whispered their verdict - junkies, inadequates, just punks. Maybe 1991 was the year that the punk broke, after all.

and the sound of seattle...

The punk/metal/pop crossover called grunge - we'll argue about the definition later - was memorably described by one critic as "the most macho, sexist development in rock for twenty years". Maybe she'd read about Mudhoney or Tad - whose beer-swilling, arm-wrestling, shit-stirring, image didn't exactly leave much room for femininity.

But she can't have seen Nirvana. At the vanguard of grunge (God I hate that word) stands the decidedly non-macho figure of Kurt Cobain. As a teenager, he delighted in accusations of homosexuality; his bisexual orientation has been admitted with candour and no sign of shame; for goodness' sake, the boy even wears a dress around the house. And he's been a vocal supporter of women's right to choose, whether the choice involves abortion or the decision to form a rock band.

Sure, his band indulge in on-stage tactics that have traditionally been classed as male - throat-searing vocals, roaring guitars, music that winds the tension tighter and tighter until it erupts into a violent thrust of sound. Plus they trash their instruments at the end of almost every show - petulant boys, perhaps, showing off the size of their royalty statements. Badmouthing the Star-Spangled Banner is one thing, but even Sinéad O'Connor never smashed a guitar.

But Kurt Cobain has never used his aggression as a sexual weapon. Check out 'Polly' on 'Nevermind' - a song which depicts the strength of a woman able to use logic and proportion to escape from that most appallingly masculine of crimes, rape. Cobain's horror when he heard that two 'fans' had recited the lyrics to 'Polly' as they raped a woman was deep and nauseous.

He married a strong woman, too - immediately transmuted by the media into an ogre, because she didn't know when to shut up (as soon as the man begins talking, apparently). The movement has already become factionalised, as progressive causes always will, but Courtney Love has become *some* kind of beacon for *some* portions of what *some* call the Riot Grrrls. Unlike some of his heroes and contemporaries, Cobain hasn't licked his lips and purred the word 'foxcore': he's simply applauded the Riot Grrrls from the beginning, encouraged his wife to make her music, apologised again and again for his gender. Maybe it's coincidence that Nirvana's non-macho ascension to male rock superstardom has been tracked by the growth of a defiantly anti-macho female rock movement, but I prefer to think of it as synchronicity.

Nirvana are just a rock band, but they've reached a level where they have a real opportunity to change the consciousness of their times. Rock fans of a certain age - up to something like 18, I suppose, and beyond that if they have little control over their own lives - take their admiration of their heroes beyond thought

EDDIE VEDDER OF PEARL JAM - THE RADIO-FRIENDLY DESCENDANTS OF THE SEATTLE PUNK SCENE.

into blind adoration. In that state, they're open vessels - open to ideas, to sounds, to persuasion, to cultural orientation. It's the undisguised power of the icon to be able to bend the minds of his fans towards his own obsessions, which is what makes Axl Rose so dangerous. Unlike Axl, Kurt Cobain thinks before he speaks, and those thoughts - liberal with that small 'l', progressive, dangerously 'left-wing' for an America dogged by the small-town prejudices of George Bush - are briefly in tune with the times, with the supposedly reborn America of Bill Clinton. President Bill wants to reform The Beatles, and they dug Fleetwood Mac and Bob Dylan up for his glitzy inauguration; his idea of nirvana doesn't quite match Cobain's. But Chelsea Clinton, and her peers, are another matter. Which could be why the politically correct rappers Arrested Development outsold all their misogynist rivals in 1992.

"I wish the Seattle scene had more political power," said local journalist Charles Cross as 'Nevermind' rose the charts. "Nirvana has a forum and I wish they had a message." Maybe Cobain was listening after all. Since then he's started to talk in interviews about men expressing their innate femininity, about the need to question the values of Republican, recession-led America, about the rights of gays and women and artists and film-makers and musicians. And the more he talks that way, the deeper those ideas are going to creep into the minds of his fans. Cobain is too laid-back to become Bono, a self-important youth prophet revelling in his own iconography. The Seattle scene has its candidates for that kind of immortality, like Pearl Jam's Eddie Vedder. But consciously or not, Cobain is influencing people - which is what makes his own fearsome struggle to overcome the titanic pressures and responsibilities of fame so important. It's too soon for conspiracy theories, perhaps, but every month that Kurt and Courtney spend locked in their apartment, or on their upstate farm, building barriers against the outside world, or fighting the latest allegations of self-abuse and child corruption, is another small victory for Axl Rose.

Cobain doesn't yet seem to have recognised his own power; he's having troubles enough surviving his media coverage. And the chances are that the mere recognition that he could remake a small percentile of the world in his own image would be enough to crack that image irrevocably. What pulls him apart from rock's would-be reformers of the past, though, from John Lennon or Bob Geldof, is that he's speaking to a constituency that politically progressive rock has never touched: the great American mass of working-class rock fans, for whom music is a point of rescue from pre-determined, barren lives. Cobain himself escaped from just such a cultural desert: for

many of his fans, Nirvana is exactly what is on offer.

And that brings us full circle, to punk, to metal, and what meaning those terms have in the 1990s. For all the national media obsession with a self-contained Seattle scene, there's little beyond geography to link Mudhoney with Pearl Jam. That's not a value judgement, merely a statement of fact. It's possible to love both bands, unless you line up behind your own choice of genre barricade, but there's no way anyone under 50 could confuse them.

Like it or not, though, both Mudhoney and Pearl Jam - or Soundgarden and Nirvana, to strike another comparison - have emerged from what is loosely called the 'alternative' music scene of Washington State. And that scene, like the State itself, is centred on Seattle. It's the largest city for miles around; it's the home of the most influential radio stations, magazines and record labels in the Pacific North-West; and it's where the small independent label, Sub Pop, issued the series of noise-racked records that altered the course of rock history. The Seattle bands are more conscious of their differences than their similarities, but to the rest of the world, the early Nineties have been dominated by the sound of Seattle. For once, the media are right: many-sided it may be, but Seattle rock does share a core identity, which couldn't have evolved anywhere else in the world.

Rock's great cities have traditionally been meeting-places. In the mid-Fifties, Memphis provided a platform where white and black cultures could cross. In the Sixties, Liverpool's location as an international port enabled the foreign sounds of American R&B to infiltrate the North of England. London and New York were the centres of mid-Seventies punk because they were cultural capitals, large enough to swallow non-conformists without spitting them out. Manchester in the late Eighties was a breeding-ground for England's indie scene, cross-fertilising the twin obsessions of guitar rock and dance music.

And Seattle? Its strength is its isolation. Another of the great Seattle clichés of recent years has been to harp on its geographical place in America, marooned in the top-left-hand corner of a country that has always been pivoted on an axis running from California to New York. "It's an isolated microcosm, not affected by any New York or Los Angeles trends," reckoned Tad frontman Tad Doyle, and there was a basic truth to his argument.

In other ways, though, Seattle - indeed, the entire Western strip of Washington State, from the mouth of the Columbia River in the South to the Strait of Juan de Fuca in the North, marking the border of Canada - has always been dependent on what happened in California.

Anyone looking for a perfect metaphor can take heart from pre-history, when the area to

the West of the Cascade mountains - which tower like a prison wall over Seattle and the other cities on Puget Sound - was a separate continent, drifting inch-by-inch from Asia to crush into the North American mainland. That separateness remains: Washington has become a haven for those who wish to stay American, but keep as far adrift from the mechanics of the Government (in that other Washington, on the Atlantic coast) as they can.

Seattle grew to be Washington State's largest city (though not its capital, which is still Olympia) because of its perfect situation. Juan de Fuca, cut like a gaping wound into the Pacific coast of the continent, twists South past islands and coves to form Puget Sound, a vast natural harbour which provided protection against marauding ships, but access to the ocean, for trade with the rest of the West Coast, and Asia beyond.

Midway down Puget Sound, in a smaller recess named Elliott Bay, was where Seattle grew up - though the first habitation didn't appear until the middle of the last century. Before that, Washington Territory had been Indian land, home of fishermen and traders, who first greeted, then violently repelled the initial imperialist invaders from Spain, Britain, Russia and finally the fledgling, Atlantic-rooted United States of America.

Aside from the Indians, who are conveniently forgotten when these kind of statements are made, it was the English who first entered Puget Sound, in 1787. George Vancouver claimed the area for the King, before the Americans arrived. After initial forays by sea, the first overland party reached the Pacific from St. Louis, headed by Lewis and Clark. By the 1830s, America was beginning to lodge settlers in the south of the territory; in 1845, England gave up its claim to the land south of the Juan de Fuca strait, and Washington Territory became American land at last.

Then, as now, the Pacific North-West was logging country. When the California Gold Rush broke in 1849, it was the making of the Washington lumber industry. The prospectors and their hangers-on - bakers, builders, whores - needed wooden cabins and offices, and the nearest source of supply was Washington. Communities built up all around Puget Sound, and one lengthy downhill timber route into the tiny community of Seattle, the site of today's Yesler Way, was named Skid Road. Within a generation that had become Skid Row, an area whose poverty and licentiousness became an American byword.

Californian businessmen made sure of their timber supplies by forming their own companies on Puget Sound; from the start, Seattle and its neighbours were effectively in thrall to California gold. Hence began the sullen, often unspoken resentment that survives to this day, the fear of Washington's natural resources being stripped

KURT COBAIN, THE FIGUREHEAD AND ARCHETYPAL
VILLAIN/HERO OF NIRVANA.

8

for profit in the evil empire two states south.

Californians weren't the only immigrants treated with mixed respect and hatred. The first wave of Chinese to reach Seattle arrived in the 1870s, providing cheap labour but failing to abandon their national culture. The locals renamed them 'Johns' - it was easier than having to tell the bastards apart, after all - but this depersonalisation wasn't enough. When there was a slump in the 1880s, the Chinese were unceremoniously herded into concentration camps and then deported. Ironically, it was the newly-formed Knights of Labor, the protectors of Washington's working-class, who led the call for their expulsion. Another template was set in place for Seattle history to repeat over and again for the next hundred years.

Another gold rush, this time in Alaska in 1897, brought back the good times to Seattle (as long as you weren't Indian or Chinese). But it took the First World War, when lumber was in desperate need for building ships and planes, to cement the city's prosperity. Boeing's first factory opened South of the metropolis, and for the next 60 years, Seattle's material fortunes ebbed and soared with the company's. Both were decimated by the slump, then boomed again during the Second World War.

Meanwhile, loggers kept tearing down the forests, caring nothing for conservation. Millions of acres of trees were felled, leaving ghastly scars across the landscape; nature, like the Indians and Chinese before it, was there to be exploited. The Second World War brought tentative moves to harness the area's resources - and another round-up of undesirable aliens, this time the Japanese, kept out of harm's way in Washington State camps (or "relocation centers", as the jargon of the time had it) until Hirohito's armies were crushed by the atomic bomb (partly built in Washington, incidentally).

With the war won, Seattle began to acquire the liberal, progressive spirit that took it to the top of those magazine polls as America's most liveable city. It built America's first modern shopping mall; ten years later, it hosted the 1962 World's Fair, which was so impressive that Elvis Presley made a dire movie about it. It left Seattle a haven of optimism, with the soaring Space Needle in the Seattle Center complex a visible symbol of its ambitions. The city spread East across Lake Washington to the sophisticated suburbs of Bellevue, while black immigrants from the South concentrated on their own less prosperous district, south of 23rd Avenue.

As testament to its modern-thinking approach, the people of Seattle began electing prominent sportsmen and TV personalities to vital city posts. By the late Eighties, they were even ready for Norm Rice, their first black mayor. But there were problems associated with the city's expansion. Geographically, the communities

DRUMMER DAVE GROHL, WHO GRADUATED TO NIRVANA FROM THE FATUOUSLY NAMED BRAIN DAMAGE.

along Puget Sound had joined tentacles, as endless suburbs spread out from Olympia in the South to Everett in the North. Seattle was still the king of Pugetopolis, as the vast urban conurbation was tagged, but that meant it also headed the region for pollution and boredom. The inter-changeable rows of houses, stretching mile after mile out of the downtown area, sapped the spirit. Seattle's reputation for dullness spread through the region: the year after *Harper's* magazine awarded the city its liveability prize, some anarchic locals spoofed the 1976 elections by forming the OWL Party who slogan was an acronym for Out With Logic, On With Lunacy. The city wasn't amused.

Culturally, Seattle had its assets - the full gamut of genteel arts, from dance to classical music, plus it was "the boating capital of the world". That was fine for a gentle drift into senior citizenship, but it left the city's under-30s bereft of inspiration. Pugetopolis had created its share of musical giants, but tradition insisted that they had to leave Washington to gain any kind of recognition. It's an impressive enough pantheon, from Bing Crosby through Ray Charles, Quincy Jones, and Jimi Hendrix.

What happened to the guru of the rock guitar is an instructive lesson in Seattle's way with hometown heroes. Born in King County Hospital in 1942, Hendrix played to black-only audiences when he began frequenting clubs in the late 50s. The city's music scene was effectively segregated back then, right down to the separate musicians' unions for whites and blacks. Jimi could get a gig at Birdland, or out on Highway 99 at the Spanish Castle, which he later immortalised in a song. But no-one was interested in capitalising on his genius - either while he was alive or dead. The Seattle music business couldn't cope with his cross-border culture-swapping; after his drug-related death, the city fathers poo-poohed any attempt to commemorate his Seattle origins. Eventually, sometime in the mid-Eighties, after the Seattle Parks Department had vetoed plans for a statue of Hendrix, he finally received his tribute: a rock, no less, positioned tactfully in the Woodland Park Zoo. Where exactly? Well, he was black, so where else but the African Savannah exhibit... tasteful, huh? So Kurt Cobain shouldn't get too excited about his chances of being mounted on a plinth when he goes.

Hendrix aside, there's a tradition of hard-edged, raw, unsophisticated rock music from Washington State. Between 1959 and 1964, when the first black radio stations were finally on air in Seattle, the North-West Sound dominated the city, plus its neighbours, and Portland, a couple of hundred miles south in Oregon. From Tacoma, just along Puget Sound, The Sonics and The Wailers were the grungiest early Sixties bands in America, putting Lou Reed's early efforts to shame. Part rock'n'roll

instrumentals, part fierce rhythm and blues, their sound was blacker and heavier than anything from California or New York. As a result, they were usually restricted to regional hits - unlike The Kingsmen and Paul Revere & The Raiders, both from Portland, and both enshrined in Sixties mythology for their primeval pre-punk recordings.

These bands played regularly enough in Seattle, but most of the city's own musicians were cover merchants - the exceptions being The Viceroys, who opted for mid-Sixties idealism as The Surprise Package, and The Daily Flash, who bridged the gap between Rolling Stones-inspired R&B and another Washington State mainstay, the folk/bluegrass scene.

Once the North-West Sound petered out - The Raiders went LA pop in the usual Washington tradition, while the rest of the bands sold out or gave up - Seattle's home-grown music scene slowly festered. In July 1969, there was a Seattle Pop Festival - actually staged across Lake Washington, in Woodinville - where Led Zeppelin, then rapidly establishing themselves as England's hottest new act, were high on the bill. But no-one formed a Seattle Nation, saving that for the hippiefest at Woodstock three weeks later.

Thereafter local talent was stymied, or else it left town. Heart moved North from California, but found a more receptive audience for their AOR over the border in Vancouver. Seattle bands kept playing covers, or recycled the banalities of LA soft-rock. And then, at last, there was punk.

What killed Seattle's mainstream rock scene was radio's refusal to get behind local bands. With a style that prided itself on its underground credentials, like punk, radio exposure beyond the colleges didn't matter. Outside London and New York, punk bands didn't judge their success by chart positions or airplay ratings: their mere existence as a poisoned thorn in the side of the rock establishment was pleasure and reward enough.

Though none of the Seattle punk bands twisted any nerves outside Washington State, the scene was vibrant enough for two or three years to support an incestuous sheaf of fanzines, all publicising records and gigs by the two dozen or so local bands who stayed together long enough to see the inside of a recording studio.
The Seattle club circuit, which had been dormant for years, came alive around 1979/80, with regular punk shows at the Basement, Showbox, Tug's Tavern, Baby O's, Astor Park, the Golden Crown and the Hall Of Fame. Besides Stephen Rabow's syndicated indie show, aired across the State, punk's bastion was the aptly named KAOS, an FM station broadcasting out of the University of

Washington in Olympia. Along with the Tone Deaf show on KUGS from Bellingham, and less regular offerings of anti-social music on stations like KCMU and KRAB, KAOS was the breathing-tube for the Seattle underground. DJs like Bruce Pavitt and Steve Fisk aired noise-crammed 45s with glee, while John Foster combined a stint at KAOS with the formation of the Lost Music Network - an information centre for Washington's indie music, and later the adopted home of Pavitt's *Sub Pop* fanzine.

Pavitt wasn't the only budding self-publisher in town. *Circle A* and *Punk Lust* maintained the strict edge of anarchy, hardcore style; Jeff Battis's *Atrophi* caught the visual iconography of the punk scene; *Attack* (motto: 'Rock against!') marshalled the troops; and there were plenty more, like *Desperate Times, Inaudible Noise, Punk Phoenix Rising* and the rest.

The bands they were eulogising, or as often as not debunking, were The Fartz and The Lewds, The Snots and The Meyce, The Beakers and The Refuzors, The Macs and Student Nurse. The Refuzors and The Fartz both copped The Ramones' gag - mock-brothers, with Messrs Blaine, Steve, Tom and Loud Fart (the drummer, of course) extending it furthest. The Refuzors' classic was 'White Power', which captures the least palatable strand of Seattle punk pretty well. The Snots weren't alone in wishing 'So Long To The Sixties', while the Lewds' anthem was 'Kill Yourself', released by the amusingly monickered Scratched Records. KAOS DJ Steve Fisk turned artist on Mr Brown Records, alongside local luminaries The Beakers, a four-piece who spawned no fewer than three spin-off bands. The Stiff Records of Seattle was Engram - home of Philippo Scrooge, The Three Swimmers, and K7s, who showed prophetic metal tendencies. Not all the Seattle new wavers sported safety pins, however: by 1981 the New Romanticism of English rock had swept up Body Falling Downstairs and Savant, both of whom sported massed synthesisers and appropriate haircuts.

The punk circuit ran from Olympia up through Seattle and its suburbs to Everett: there were even sightings of Mohicans as far east as Spokane, across the other side of the Cascades. But there was no outlet for Washington's music beyond the state borders, save for an occasional jaunt into Canada. And even within the Western strip - 100 miles South-West of Seattle, for example, in Aberdeen - there were corners where the punk rhetoric just wouldn't fit.

It was in Aberdeen, on February 20, 1967, that Kurt Cobain was born. Imagine yourself 100 miles out of London, New York or Los Angeles, and the focal point of your existence would still be the big city. But Aberdeen, and its sister town Hoquiam, cherished their independence and isolation.

KURT COBAIN "SPENT THE FIRST TWO DECADES OF HIS LIFE IN AN OASIS".

There are three roads out of Aberdeen, and two of those are dead ends. The third leads towards Olympia, and on to Seattle, and that was the path Cobain took. But not until he was almost twenty years old: he spent the first two decades of his life in an oasis.

The same logging industry that fired Pugetopolis brought inhabitants to Grays Harbor, a Pacific coast inlet that leads past Rennie Island into Chehalls River. In the 1880s, settlers first began to sacrifice the woods that surrounded the harbour, tapping the almost limitless natural resources of this deserted region. At the mouth of the harbour, they built a boom town, Grays Harbor City, with the grandiose aim of toppling Seattle as Washington Territory's largest town. Within two years, the boom had bust, and Grays Harbor City was left a ghost village made out of the very timber it had been built to exploit.

That site is now part of the grandly named Ocean City State Park - a brave attempt to turn the windswept, rain-moistened Pacific coast into a pleasure beach. Thermal underwear is a necessity; Ocean City State Park is no more Hawaii than Aberdeen is a metropolis. And at around 19,000 people, with another nine or ten thousand alongside the harbour in Hoquiam, a metropolis is not what's on offer in Grays Harbor.

The blandishments of Ocean City aside, Aberdeen is somewhere you leave, not arrive. When Kurt Cobain described it as "a dead logging town on the shores of the Pacific Ocean... *Twin Peaks* without the excitement", he wasn't underselling it. What passes for entertainment in Aberdeen is Undiscovery Day in late April, which - a neat touch, this - commemorates the time when Captain George Vancouver failed to investigate Grays Harbor on his way to Juan de Fuca. Those residents with a lively sense of irony rush down to the beach at midnight, and shout "Hey George" to the waves. It doesn't exactly pull the tourists in.

Otherwise, there are bars and clubs - a run of pubs and restaurants on Heron Street, close to the river, and a couple of branches of the local cheap-and-easy eatery, the pie specialists Duffy's, one each end of what passes for downtown. Duffy's East is on the road to Olympia, past the local convention centre and what would be a tourist attraction if there were any tourists, the Grays Harbor Historical Seaport. Turn right out of town before you get that far, and you hit Aberdeen's landmark - the river bridge, which takes locals down to Safeway, and the South Shore Mall, home of the local K Mart. Or stay East for Wishkah Mall, and Pay'N'Save. Or stay home and brood about the recession, and its savage effect on the local lumber trade.

When the Grays Harbor Commercial Company, centre of the logging industry in Aberdeen around the turn of this century, first caught wind that local workers were joining the socialist union movement, the Wobblies, they policed the yards with alsatians and armed guards, to keep the people in their place. Something of that grim undercurrent of violence remains - as it probably does in every backwoods American town which the main currents of the century have passed by. "Every state has its Aberdeen", Cobain has said; he was unfortunate enough to be raised in Washington's.

The town had never been rich, but economic hardship arrived in the mid-Seventies - around the time that Kurt Cobain's parents divorced. It's a myth that Washington State has an abnormally high suicide rate. No-one disputes that the incidence of mental illness and nervous disorder in Aberdeen and Hoquiam is out of the ordinary, though. The economy is much to blame - that and the sense that nothing is ever going to shake the town out of its mild depression. "They've been through a lot of hard times," says insider/outsider (and Nirvana bassist) Chris Novoselic, who came to the town in his teens. "When the economy goes down, less homes are being built, there's less lumber going out. It's like the edge. There's Seattle, Olympia, Aberdeen, then *China*. No ideas are going through. There's a collective unconscious there." And Cobain himself describes the daily round: "chopping down trees, drinking, having sex and drinking, talking about sex and drinking some more. There's not a lot of enthusiasm among the people of this town, they don't want to do anything. There's a massive sense of depression - and alcoholism. There's this overall sense that we're a little ashamed of our roots."

For the first nine years of his life, Kurt Cobain escaped the grim realities of Aberdeen into childhood fantasy - conversations with his imaginary friend Boda, singing wherever he went, listening to The Beatles over and over again. His mother, Wendy O'Connor, who was variously a cocktail waitress and a secretary, recalled: "He got up every day with such joy that there was another day to be had. When we'd go downtown to the stores, he would sing to people. He was focused on the world."

Kurt's father was an auto machinist; they lived "in a two-storey house, lower middle class family". "I had a really good childhood up until I was nine years old," Kurt remembered. "Then a classic case of divorce really affected me and I moved back and forth between relatives all the time. And I just became really depressed and withdrawn." For two years, Kurt lived with his father in a trailer-park; then he was passed from cousins to grandparents. "It just destroyed his life," his mother admitted. "He changed completely. I think he was ashamed. And he became very inward - he just held everything back. He became real shy. I think he's still suffering."

For a snapshot of Cobain's internalised terror,

listen to 'Sliver', Nirvana's remarkable between-albums single. "Mom and dad go off somewhere and leave the kid with his grandparents," he summarised when asked to explain the song. "He gets confused and frightened, he doesn't understand what's happening." But that scarcely touched the jagged emotions of the song, or the frenzied hysteria of Cobain's vocal. And then ponder his throwaway comments about his grandfather, and think about the balance of fiction and fact: "My grandpa's a dick. He used to play racist jokes. He looks like Brezhnev. He's got colon cancer. He deserves it."

As he entered his teens, Kurt gradually shut down his contacts with the outside world: "I felt alienated, I started feeling confused. I couldn't understand why I didn't want to hang out with the kids at school. Years later I realised why - I didn't relate to them because they didn't appreciate anything artistic or cultural. In Aberdeen, 99% of people had no idea what music was. Or art. It was their bread to become loggers. And I was a small kid, really small, which was why I didn't want to go into the logging industry."

Alienation had its limits: maybe because he wasn't an obvious jock, obsessed with male bonding, he collected a little cabal of female admirers: "The cheerleaders thought I was cute. The jocks would try to befriend me because they knew the jock-girls thought I was cute. I just chose not to hang around with them." Elsewhere, he summed up his teenage ideology in a single sentence: "It was really fun to fuck with people all the time."

Part of that fucking involved, appropriate enough, experimenting with sexual identities beyond the jock-stereotype which passed for orthodox Aberdeen. He found making friends with girls easy, but "I didn't find any of the girls in my high school attractive. They had really awful haircuts and fucked-up attitudes. So I thought I would try to be gay for a while."

By 1981, the year when he got his first guitar, Cobain had turned alienation and ambivalence into some kind of art-form: "I've had the reputation of being a homosexual ever since I was 14. It was really cool, because I found a couple of gay friends in Aberdeen - which was almost impossible. I got beat up a lot, of course, because of my association with them. People just thought I was weird, at first, just some fucked-up kid. But once I got the gay tag, it gave me the freedom to be able to be a freak and let people know they should stay away from me. It made for quite a few scary experiences in alleys walking home from school, too."

"This town is just like Peyton Place," his mother explains. "Everybody is watching and judging, and they have their little slots they like everyone to stay in - and he didn't." So he created his own, and embellished it: from the

age of 12, he wanted to be a rock'n'roll star.

The family tree histories of rock'n'roll are sensible enough, I suppose. From the vantage point of the 21st century, anyone keen enough to look back at the 1980s will decide that, of course, New York punk inspired London punk, which in turn sparked American hardcore, which merged with Seventies hard rock, glam and Eighties death metal to produce grunge.

With hindsight and a suitably wide record collection, that theory makes sense. What it ignores is that history is not just mass movements; it's just as much the collective story of individuals. And individuals, especially 13-year-olds living on the edge of America 70 miles from the nearest city, don't have access to the entire recorded history of Western popular music.

So Kurt Cobain's musical development isn't as linear or as obvious as the theory might suggest. He was restricted by what his parents had around the house - The Beatles, The Monkees, The Chipmunks. Then, when he was sharing the trailer with his dad, there was the record club which delivered regular doses of hard rock - Zeppelin, Kiss, Aerosmith, Sabbath. During the punk maelstrom, Cobain was marooned in the early Seventies. But he read about punk, following the Sex Pistols' devilish path across American through the teen-rock mags, and trying to imagine in his head, and on his first guitar, what they must sound like. In late 1981, he finally tracked down someone in Aberdeen who owned a punk record - or what should have been a punk record - the Clash's sprawling, eclectic, bloated triple-album experiment, *Sandinista*. Cobain was mortified: no guitar riffs, no anger, no catharsis. "I blame *Sandinista* for not letting me get into punk, years after I should have done," he noted in 1991. "It was so bad."

Starved for the moment of external inspiration, Cobain created his own: "I started working on songwriting right away when I got a guitar, rather than learn a bunch of Van Halen covers. I had to develop my own style. I only know a couple of cover songs to this day, and they're the ones I learned when I first had the guitar - 'My Best Friend's Girl' by The Cars and Zeppelin's 'Communication Breakdown'."

Aberdeen had bars, and Aberdeen had bands, but all of them played covers - all, that was, except one. Matt Lukin (bass), Dale Crover (drums) and Buzz Osborne (guitar and vocals) were Aberdeen's authentic punks. One day they read a story in the local rag about a 50-year-old man called Melvin who'd been caught stealing Christmas trees from the Montesano Thriftway. Even for Aberdeen, it was a singularly desperate and pointless crime; and it appealed to the band, who duly christened themselves The Melvins.

That was around 1981, though it was a couple

15

of years before they began gigging on a regular basis. Unlike the rest of Aberdeen, they'd been exposed to America's second wave of punk and the birth of hardcore, and they started out playing proto-Ramones rants - race-you-to-the-end dirges about frustration, stupidity and angst. But despite their lip service to punk, The Melvins were early Seventies children. Buzz Osborne admitted later to listening to "nothing after 1979, and that's pushing it. Our sound came from years of only listening to Kiss and living in Grays Harbor." Besides Kiss, the cartoon mock-monsters whose theatricals on-and off-stage thrilled American teenies, while outraging all rock critics except Lester Bangs, The Melvins idolised other fathers of excess, like Black Sabbath (grunge metal fifteen years too soon) and Ted Nugent (redneck imagery crossed with Motor City madness).

"Everybody hated us everywhere we played in Aberdeen," Osborne remembers. "Then it was real cool to be super fast, and we just weren't like that at all. People weren't into it. We went for a long time with nobody liking us."

Well, not quite nobody. At 14 or 15, searching for male heroes to establish his own masculinity, and needing a rapid infusion of punk attitude, Kurt Cobain was enthralled by these magazine heroes come to life in his own backyard. In everything but sex, he became a Melvins groupie - watching literally hundreds of rehearsals, stacking amps into their van, gazing adoringly from side-stage while the band plodded through their dirge-like metal mantras to indifferent audiences. "I remember when we started," says Buzz Osborne, "that we'd be lucky to play to 30 or 40 people."

For Cobain, that was stardom enough. The mere existence of the band proved a point: "We didn't exist in a backwater after all," he recalled. "We had the Melvins in our town, and we used to go and listen to them rehearse all the time." And by this time he wasn't alone. In 1984, just after Kurt had finished high school, Buzz Osborne introduced him to a kid two years older, and eight inches or more taller - 18-year-old Chris Novoselic.

For three years, Novoselic had been experiencing culture shock. Born on May 16, 1965, and raised by his Croatian parents in the Los Angeles suburb of Compton, he'd been uprooted at the age of 15 when his father's job in the logging business led him to "screwy" Grays Harbor. In Aberdeen, no-one at school liked the same music as Novoselic - Led Zeppelin, Devo, Kiss, and Black Flag. While his mother settled sedately into their new hometown, opening a hairdressing salon called Maria's Hair Design, Chris dropped out of school to work as a fisherman. In between jobs, he painted bridges - anything to fill the gap between excursions to Tacoma and Seattle, to see punk shows.

It was only natural that Cobain and Novoselic,

both feeling like outcasts from blinkered Aberdeen youth culture, should gravitate towards the town's established rebels - the Melvins.

"Buzz Osborne and Matt Lukin discovered punk rock," Chris recalled. "They'd go to Seattle and catch all these cool shows and buy records. I told Buzz, 'I play guitar', and he started turning me on to all these bands, like Flipper, MDC and The Butthole Surfers. I thought it was really cool. Then I tried turning other people onto this stuff, but I'd just get all these closed-mind reactions. One guy said: 'All that stuff's just "I wanna fuck my mom".' "

The previous year, Matt Lukin had taken Kurt Cobain to see his first real live show - Black Flag in Seattle. "He was blown away," Lukin remembered. "After that, he was always trying to start bands, but it was hard to find people who wouldn't flake out on him." "Chris never had an interest to be in a band, I think," says Cobain, "but I'd been looking for people to jam with for years."

So was born Ed, Ted and Fred - a three-piece, naturally enough, with Cobain on drums, Novoselic on guitar, and a bassist called Steve. "Then he cut his fingers off in a logging accident," explained Kurt gleefully: whatever, he vanished leaving Kurt and Chris to jam with whichever of The Melvins was around, or to drag in other locals to play Creedence Clearwater Revival covers in local bars.

During the day, Cobain hustled for money, picking up work wherever he could. Quitting high school put an end to his mother's ambitions to send him to college, and in disgust at his lack of commitment to his studies, and the company he was keeping, she kicked him out. For one summer, he camped under the bridge which linked Aberdeen with its mall-infested suburb, Cosmopolis - Chris painted it by day, Kurt slept under it at night. Or else he bummed a night's sleep on someone's couch - until Matt Lukin took him in as a permanent flatmate. Kurt swept floors in one of Aberdeen's handful of guest houses, and then graduated to janitor at a dentists' surgery. Briefly, it threatened to become a career: "I was in charge of driving the truck round to all these doctors' and dentists' offices and cleaning them. I was my own boss, too."

Making a career entailed some kind of social responsibility, and Kurt Cobain didn't view Aberdeen as being worth the effort. Out on the streets at night with Novoselic, he took to spray-painting provocative slogans across the town - on trucks, shop fronts, business offices. "That was a lot of fun," he recalled. "The funniest thing was not actually the act, but the next morning. I'd get up early to walk through the neighbourhood that I'd terrorised, to see the aftermath." And he wasn't spraying 'Black Flag Rules'. The story improves with each retelling, but the thrust of Cobain's impromptu messages

was iconoclastic. 'God is Gay', perhaps ("that was the worst thing I could ever have spray-painted on their cars"), 'Queer' or 'Abort Christ'. One night in 1985, Cobain, Novoselic and Osborne blasted a slogan onto the side of a bank in downtown Aberdeen. When the local police interrupted them, Chris and Buzz hid in an alley: Cobain was left holding the can, with his MDC punk cassette in his pocket as an identity badge. He was fined $180 and given a 30-day suspended sentence for vandalism. And the offensive slogan? Cobain says it was 'Homosexual Sex Rules'. Osborne, more prosaically, remembers it as 'Quiet Riot'. The best tales always grow taller by the year.

Through 1985 and into 1986, Cobain and Novoselic kept performing - Ed, Ted and Fred became Skid Row, even at one point Fecal Matter, though it's unlikely they ever played in Aberdeen under that name. Kurt was aware that this wasn't enough: "I always wanted to experience street life because my teenage life in Aberdeen was so boring. I wanted to move to Seattle, find a chicken hawk - an older gay man - sell my ass and be a punk rocker. But I was too afraid. So I just stayed in Aberdeen - for too long."

Still equating his misfit status in his hometown with homosexuality, Cobain never had to sell himself on the street - though the image stuck, and a *Rolling Stone* reporter visiting the town after 'Nevermind' came out found school contemporaries willing to swear that "the Cobain kid's a faggot". As Matt Lukin recalls, "Kurt was terrified of jocks and moron dudes", and in Aberdeen they were the norm.

Besides fucking with their minds and their shopfronts, Cobain enjoyed some private revenge with his songwriting - filling his earliest compositions with vignettes of Aberdeen life, character assassinations of local stereotypes. Persuading the populace to listen was another matter. Novoselic remembers playing "in this shitty old house, in front of five people. Everybody would be drunk or stoned." And Cobain confirms that "No one liked it." But no-one liked The Melvins much in Aberdeen either, and yet in 1986 - on February 8, to be exact - they cut an album in Seattle. It was slow, grinding, totally uncompromising. Kurt was impressed - and intrigued.

The outrage that greeted The Melvins' decision to sit resolutely in first gear was rooted in the rigid commandments of the punk gospel. And although they claimed no allegiance to music beyond 1979, The Melvins were still - in attitude, at least - punks.

For punk in Britain, 1976 was Year Zero. "No Elvis, Beatles or Rolling Stones, in 1977," sang the Clash, and at that point they were still looking into the future. Year One was when the punk culture slapped the mainstream in the face - when the London police raided the Pistols'

NIRVANA'S DEBUT ALBUM PERSONNEL WITH DRUMMER CHAD CHANNING ON LEFT.

COURTNEY LOVE, THE 'DRAGON LADY' OF THE
SEATTLE ROCK MYTH.

jolly boating jaunt down the Thames, when Rotten, Cook and Jones were attacked on the streets, when the charts were manipulated to make sure that 'God Save The Queen' wasn't No. 1 the week of the Royal Jubilee. Slipping The Adverts and The Boomtown Rats onto *Top Of The Pops* seemed like some kind of victory back then, although it was a short step from Bob Geldof sneering at the camera lens to tourist kiosks and their racks of cute London punks, neatly packaged on 5" by 3" postcards. Punk was a caricature, heading full-speed ahead for cartoon status.

The London rock scene slurps up revolutions like a dog afraid each meal might be its last. By 1978, punk had been co-opted into New Wave - sharp-suited, bootlace-tied refugees from the pub circuit, reheating the clichés of The Beatles and the Stones with extra guitars and a lip-snarl. Splinters of the briefly united punk movement began to dart in all directions - a Mod revival, all anoraks and scooters, wishing it could be 1965 again; power pop, John, Paul, George and Ringo without the ambition; the avant-garde, deconstructing every convention in sight but unable to decide what - if anything - to build in the ruins.

The first whiff of betrayal was in the air, though no-one was sure who'd betrayed whom. Those who'd looked to punk to overthrow the state, or at least challenge its power structures, drifted into single-issue campaigns - against the bomb, racism, sexism, fascism - each capable of filling a London park, but increasingly preaching to the converted.

Across the other side of the chasm were the True Punks - addicted to a single snapshot as a totem for future generations. These were the people for whom the picture postcards were real: as long as they kept their hair spiky and spat vigorously at bands, the world was still creeping in their direction. Conservativism breeds conservatism, and soon the Campaign for Real Punk became a campaign to keep Britain Great - and White. The self-proclaimed Oi! movement thrived on its oppositional stance, at the same time as it shored up the most reactionary principles of the British Empire. By the time that punks were fighting mods, and the Art School crowd were writing manifestoes and theses, *en route* to the New Romanticism of the Eighties, anyone with power to lose in 1977 must have been sniggering behind their suit-cuffs. "Punk's not dead", screamed the traditionalists, proving that it was already six feet under.

There was, even at this stage, an alternative - in the vitality and non-conformism of the fledgling indie scene. Encompassing college graduates and ex-hippies as easily as schoolgirls and drop-outs, it picked up on punk's initial refusal to be co-opted by establishment values, and carried the stance through to its consequences. Outrage mattered

less than self-expression, and the indie scene's open-minded approach to musical genres briefly inspired a startling merging of styles, with free-form jazz and reggae sitting alongside pop and traditional punk, often all on the same record. This was punk's most exciting offspring, but the spirit of eclecticism scarcely survived beyond 1981, dampened by the hard realities of commercial logic.

In America, punk hadn't come close to capturing the mainstream, or even its attention, so there was less to lose when the initial explosion conformed to expectations - and exploded. Out in Washington State, Kurt Cobain read about the Pistols in '78, but didn't get to hear them, or The Clash, for another three or four years. Six thousand miles from London, the stylistic minutiae which divided the post-punk cults were effectively meaningless: what happened in Britain was inspiring, but didn't begin to set an example.

Neither, for those outside LA and San Francisco, did New York punk. Its London cousin was built around aspects of the New York scene - the Ramones' steamroller approach to songwriting, Richard Hell's affectation of vacant expressions, ripped T-shirts and spiked hair, the New York Dolls' post-glam swagger. But the prime movers of the New York new wave were Artists. Patti Smith and Television's Tom Verlaine wrote poetry; Smith had been mixing with film-makers and photographers since the Warhol years. Their revulsion at what passed for culture in the mid-Seventies was authentic enough, but their revolution was cultivated, not organic. For all the art-house crowd who flocked to Greenwich Village to experience the electric shock of punk, New York new wave made more impact on experimentalists in Britain than it did on teenage rock'n'roll in the States. The Ramones and Richard Hell had to export their comedy routines to London, and then watch them being shipped back to the American heartland as another British Invasion.

Smith, Television, Hell and the rest wielded massive power on the New York underground; and when that punk intelligence - filtered through British acts like the Fall, Wire and Public Image Ltd - met the garage-punk/art-college leanings of Sonic Youth, then somehow the sound that resulted was marketed as punk again. But that was a decade down the road: in the late Seventies, punk survived in America only in major cities, where British singles by the Pistols, The Damned and The Clash could be tracked down as imports, and where some tiny vanguard of the English revolution might make tentative inroads into the local club scene.

As early as 1977, the first stirrings of an American response to the Pistols were apparent in New York and California - particularly on the West Coast, where Black Flag formed the SST label to market themselves. Unstable in

personnel, scattershot when it came to their musical approach, the Flag still came closer than any other American band to creating an American Pistols. On their first EP, they crammed two years of British punk into the fifty seconds of 'Wasted'; there was nothing more they needed to say. And by 1981, when they cut the playful, savage 'Damaged' album, they had turned a British art-form into an American cultural statement, with songs like 'Six-Pack' and 'TV Party' satirising and celebrating the bored, semi-affluent existence of big-city teenage wastrels.

For a couple of years, especially when Henry Rollins became Black Flag's lyricist and frontman, the band encapsulated the West Coast punk sound. Then they fragmented, holding too many preoccupations for any two-minute rant to bear. Rollins started reciting his poetry while the band played instrumentals; it was the beatniks all over again. As the Flag broadened their horizons, so the centre began to capsize under the excess weight. They made great music after 1982, but it was punk only in name and spirit.

Jello Biafra's Dead Kennedys handled much of the slack, towering over the American punk scene for the early years of the Eighties. In Biafra, they had a figurehead who was soon looking beyond cartoon imagery for real power and influence. On their first album, *Fresh Fruit For Rotting Vegetables*, their deliberately provocative monicker concealed a fierce political intelligence. For the Kennedys, being Punk wasn't enough: they wanted to change California, and then the world. They weren't totalitarian about it, though Biafra did made a well-publicised (and amazingly well-supported) run for Mayor in San Francisco. But their music was about their message, and sometimes the ironic insight of Biafra's lyrics slipped over the heads of the band's punk following.

1982 was the year when the weight of the Flag and the Kennedys dumped a generation of American punk bands onto the market. By this time, the initial flash of British punk 45s had reached every city in the country, and the time was ripe for some kind of reaction against the anti-thought, pro-conformism rock that was being offered by the major labels.

Fanzines like San Francisco's *Maximum Rock'n'Roll* were there to document the fall-out. Chief contributor Tim Yohannan explains: "My theory on rock'n'roll goes something like this. First you get the pure stuff, be it 1957, 1965, 1977 or 1982. These are 'outburst' years, when the finest grade of musical adrenalin hits the streets. Total lift-off! Within two or three years, the whole thing disintegrates. Some people OD on the real McCoy, get sick of the straight goods. Some people become 'musicians' and want to exercise their talent by getting eclectic, experimenting, or regressing to their 'pre-punk' roots. Some people see dollar signs in watering down the material so it can have more mass consumption.

"The first wave of modern punk died an ugly death by 1980, when the original bands went 'post-punk, slowing down, adding extraneous rhythms and arty pretensions, incorporating disco, new wave and Seventies rock into a new 'progressive' artform. By 81/82, a new crew of kids came along, saw the bullshit for what it was, and began a new whole period of mainline punk - called hardcore punk."

Like the British punk scene before it, hardcore incorporated a bewildering range of beliefs - from Nazism to Marxism, excess to celibacy, social change to anti-social behaviour. But from 1982 onwards, the heart of hardcore was acutely moral: punk was not just a nihilistic style, it was a cause. Often it was self-generating - punks campaigning for punk, nothing more. But at its most (or maybe I should say least) extreme, it became a rigid order of beliefs, a self-contained religion with no god beyond the temple of the body and the mind.

The result was 'straight edge' - a punk movement that had no impact beyond the denizens of the hardcore scene in America, but which became a guiding philosophy for a generation of intensely serious-minded bands. The title came from a song by Washington DC's Minor Threat, which called for an end to indulgence in dope, guns and booze: as the movement developed, the abstinence extended to sex, thereby covering the entire gamut of activities which punk had originally set out to celebrate.

Minor Threat eventually capsized under the burden they had chosen to carry as self-appointed martyrs to the revolution. But the Positive Core ethic survived via bands like Youth Of Today, who focused on the consumption of meat as one of society's burning evils, and reiterated their opposition to drugs and alcohol. (Youth Of Today frontman Ray Cappo eventually joined the Krishna movement, which perhaps wasn't quite what Sid Vicious had in mind.)

With Henry Rollins and Black Flag joining the clarion call for belief in yourself and your principles (right down to his self-improvement rap of late 1992, 'Low Self Opinion'), rock's anarchic wing had been hijacked for the pursuit of Knowing Thyself and Doing Good Deeds. In the heartlands, this ascetic mood wasn't always received with enthusiasm.

Reformed excessives always make the best celibates, as they know the power of what they're rejecting. Living in a community that offered nothing but the narrowest form of conformism, a teenager like Kurt Cobain could hardly be expected to embrace the new morality with enthusiasm. "That was really the time when hardcore was very big in America - this straight edge, very philosophical type of music," he explained after Nirvana's first album was

released. "They don't have sex, they don't smoke cigarettes, they don't think. It's fine if somebody wants to do that, to promote it to such an extreme, but it's offensive to me. The hardcore bands made me want to rebel against the very typical form of punk at that time. I tried to find other bands that were subversive to that kind of music. Flipper, Scratch Acid and The Butthole Surfers were completely the opposite to the straight edge scene - they were very much more like 1977 punk rock, when things were a bit more open. It was punk, but anti-hardcore."

From Flipper to The Melvins was only a short trip. The San Francisco band took the same route as Aberdeen's finest, slowing the pulse-racing tempo of hardcore down to a piledriver. The band weren't offering any thrills - they had two bassists, for god's sake, and a musical style like the last lumbering steps of a dinosaur on the verge of distinction. The anti-straight edge lifestyle took its toll - Flipper bassist Will Shatter overdosed on heroin in 1987 - but their noise-soaked, deeply intense music carried its own emotional power.

Kurt Cobain's other heroes came from that bastion of outsiderness, Austin, Texas. Scratch Acid revelled in noise - sometimes twisted into recognisable songs, more often an ear-closing barrage of sound that melded layers of shrieking guitars to the cat-like, beyond-hysterical squawl of (the aptly named) David Yow's vocals. Rising from a scream to a tortured howl in a matter of seconds, Yow taught Cobain that the human voice could be as much an instrument of oppression as any squeal or buzz of guitar feedback.

From fellow Austinites, The Butthole Surfers, Cobain picked up similar lessons. Gibby Haynes screeched on their records - "I'm not fucking kidding, man, it hurts," he wailed on the proto-Nirvana Buttholes classic, 'Suicide'. And the band thrashed like animals trapped in a forest fire behind him. At other moments, The Butthole Surfers abandoned reason for the playroom, dragging together mean parodies of the rock scene, burbling schoolboy humour, sudden cascades of noise, all determinedly lacking in significance. For a boy raised in a logging town, the mere existence of a band like that had to provide some kind of liberation.

Of these three influences, The Buttholes contributed anarchic freedom to Cobain's musical vision, Scratch Acid unlocked his voice, and Flipper (as diverted via The Melvins, themselves veterans of the descent from manic speed to eerie crawl), the framework. From the past, he couldn't escape the melodic precision of The Beatles - but it was another British band who sealed the circle.

Universally derided among the British rock cognoscenti for the best part of two decades, Black Sabbath are finally being admitted - with extreme reluctance - to the underground rock

KURT COBAIN AND MUDHONEY'S MARK ARM CROSS THE GREAT DIVIDE. NIRVANA'S SUCCESS EVENTUALLY DRAGGED MUDONEY INTO THE MAJOR LABEL LEAGUE.

hall of fame, where they sit uneasily alongside The Velvet Underground, The Stooges and The MC5.

Of all 20th century rehabilitations, Sabbath's was the least predictable. In the wake of the late Sixties' power trios like the Hendrix Experience, Cream, Blue Cheer and (moving ever closer to the ridiculous) Mountain, Black Sabbath seemed to represent a new nadir. Their deadening, deadened metal appealed to the teenage working-class in Britain's most industrialised cities, where its non-liberating sonic assault worked as an unholy metaphor for its listeners' lives. The same rock critics who were prepared to countenance that Mick Jagger might be the Devil's son dismissed Ozzy Osborne's Satanic leanings as so much hype, and although no-one could quite deny the impact of an occasional Sabbath song, like the 1970 hit 'Paranoid', no-one with intelligence to protect was likely to own up to their influence in public.

As in Britain, though, American teenagers for whom California hippiedom was a luxury that they couldn't afford responded to Sabbath's gloom and power - just as they did to the post-blues boom hard rock of Led Zeppelin, dismissed as exploitation merchants by the Sixties critical elite. Allied to the pre-punk imagery of Iggy Pop and The Stooges, Black Sabbath's pounding, unrelenting rhythms matched the tempo of teenage life.

All this noise - The Melvins, Black Sabbath, Black Flag, The Sex Pistols, Led Zeppelin, Flipper, Scratch Acid, The Butthole Surfers - congealed in Kurt Cobain's mind, and formed his fantasy of what a punk rock band should sound like in 1984. It wasn't right for the streets of Aberdeen - where, as Buzz Osborne of The Melvins noted, "It's so backward, it's forward. There are only cover bands here, so we have no real competition." And The Melvins, don't forget, still weren't reaching a local audience beyond their friends' friends.

Beyond Aberdeen, though, North-East to the college town of Olympia and beyond to Washington's Mecca, Seattle, there were people willing to listen. Seattle, for the moment, remained difficult to conquer. Buzz Osborne again: "You go to Tacoma or Olympia and the people there are a lot more starved for attention. You don't have overkilled music like you do in Seattle. It's more of a special thing. Pretty much everybody who goes to shows goes to almost every show."

So it was Olympia, home of Evergreen State College, that The Melvins conquered first - and where Kurt Cobain's band, still sliding from one name to the next on a monthly basis, played their first out-of-town shows. But, as Kurt recalled, "Our big goal was still to play in Seattle one day."

"We were a band for a year and a half before we even played there," says Chris Novoselic.

"We never knew about any Seattle scene. We were real naive about the whole thing."

Naïvety was pretty much in keeping with the higher echelons of the Seattle rock underground in the first half of the Eighties. The lack of commercial success eventually crushed the city's punk and hardcore scene: by 1984, almost none of the punk pioneers of five years' earlier were still intact, and anyway, there was no club scene left for them to play. A year earlier, Seattle journalist Dawn Anderson had launched a magazine called *Backfire* which, she recalled, "attempted to break some barriers by featuring bands like Mötley Crüe alongside bands like DOA". Her prophetic vision of a hybrid of glam metal and hardcore punk came about too late to save *Backfire*, which went down after just five issues. (Anderson tried again a few years later with *Backlash*, which was more successful but still went out of business on the verge of Nirvana's breakthrough in 1991.)

As far as the outside world was concerned, Seattle in the early Eighties was the home of the Young Fresh Fellows, introduced on Conrad Uno's PopLlama label in 1982. Their witty, college-boy blend of sharply-written pop songs and soundbites - epitomised via song titles like 'You've Got Your Head On Backwards' and 'I Got My Mojo Working (And I Thought You'd Like To Know)' - had little if anything in common with the punk scene, but its 'alternative' status meant that it had to feed on the underground media and distribution circuit as the grunge bands would later.

Beat Happening, who emerged around the same time, and had a much more lasting influence on what happened in Seattle, were also far removed from Black Sabbath and Scratch Acid. They brought a slightly manic edge to the 3,000-miles-removed New York punk sound of the Velvets, as translated by Jonathan Richman. All of that meant that their songs were powerful without being heavy, clever without being annoyingly smart, and usually tailored towards recognisable pop formats.

Elsewhere, on the pre-recording contract underground, there were what Mark Arm of Mudhoney calls... "the two I's - isolation and inbreeding. There was this one corner of the map that was busy being in-bred and ripping off each other's ideas." Arm would become a central figure in the Seattle grunge scene, though not before exhausting some other obsessions - by recording an EP with his first band, Mr. Epp & The Calculations, that sounded distinctly 'New Wave' (not punk), and posing for group photos as a bunch of gawky Devo impersonators. The title of their record reflected their Devoist philosophy: 'Of Course I'm Happy. Why?'

Elsewhere in Seattle, 14-year-old Andrew

Wood had formed a band called Malfunkshun as early as 1980 - little realising he'd be locked into the same incestuous family tree as Mark Arm eight years later, and dead within ten. Arm's Mr Epp formed a year later, alongside a brother outfit called The Limp Richards - a joke band from the start, but one which introduced Mark Arm to fellow guitarist Steve Turner. (Like Kurt Cobain, Arm actually started out a drummer and ended up a grunge vocalist.) Turner was active in another band, The Ducky Boys, who played glam-metal and included another promising guitar player, Stone Gossard.

Chronicling these club-circuit bands with anything like precision is virtually impossible - and irrelevant too, as their floating line-ups are replicated in any major city rock scene. Only distant historians will care, for instance, that The Ducky Boys disintegrated around 1983, bequeathing Steve Turner (and fellow Limp Richard, guitarist Charles Guain) to a band called Spluii Numa (catchy, huh?). Or that meanwhile, Turner, who was obviously promiscuous in his loyalties, also ended up in the second generation of Mr Epp, fresh from their local-label EP and looking for a new identity away from the 'Are We Not Devo/No You Are Mr Epp' tag.

What matters is their next move, from these casual rock groupings to their first committed attempt at Seattle stardom: Green River. This band evolved in 1984, Mark Arm and Steve Turner dragging in out-of-towner Jeff Ament ("serious Montana skate punk with a Marshall", as he described himself years later) and Spluii Numa drummer Alex Vincent. Cutting demos that fall, of songs like '10,000 Things' and '33RPM', Green River sounded like Aerosmith crossed with Blue Cheer - generic hard rock with a metallic edge, overshadowed by the fearsome roar of Mark Arm's rasping voice. Already, though, they were very much A Band - focused on their music in a way which had eluded their earlier incarnations.

Boosted by local radio stations like the University's KCMU in Olympia, and KJET, and playing a circuit of clubs like the Rainbow Tavern, the Gorilla Gardens and Squid Row, Green River and their cohorts built up a strong following across Pugetopolis. That needs to be put in perspective, though: their alternative market paled alongside the rapidly growing fan base for the city's pure metal scene, headed by Queensryche (who leaped from local notoriety to international stardom within four years, and by 1989 were racking up record sales that could be counted in millions) and the less successful but still immensely popular Metal Church. A sign of the times was that Queensryche hadn't even played a single live show when they signed their major label deal: they'd simply sent out a four-track demo. Faced with that kind of competition, and the knowledge that the Seattle hardcore scene had recently expired for lack of exposure, the new breed of hard rock/punk bands can have had few realistic ambitions of escaping over the state borders.

What the new troupe of Seattle bands shared, beyond limited expectations, was a vision of excess. Fuelled by the glam-metal of Mötley Crüe and Kiss, linked to the leaden punk of Flipper and the later Black Flag, the likes of Green River, Malfunkshun, The Melvins, The U-Men, Soundgarden and Skin Yard all played real, real slow. But they weren't dour, not for a moment. There was plenty of make-up on the scene - not for nothing do Green River's early publicity shots look like a bizarre cross-breed of The New York Dolls and a bunch of poodles. And there was posing a-plenty, particularly from the scene's two most charismatic front men, Andrew Wood and Soundgarden's Chris Cornell.

Andrew Wood first told his brother Kevin that he wanted to be a rock star after seeing Kiss perform in Seattle in 1977. Wood was then 11: three years later, the two brothers began to experiment with a cheap tape recorder and copy guitars. Their next convert was Regan Hagar, who duly became the third member of Malfunkshun in the early Eighties. "Playing in Malfunkshun with Andy was like we had a mission to spread the word of love," beamed Hagar a decade later. "We were the opposite of all the bands that were heavy and Satanic."

Forget the Black Sabbath comparisons, then: Malfunkshun's metal was always glamorous, polished until the self-obsessed Andy Wood could admire his own reflection. Though the band initially shared club bills with the likes of The Fartz, their shameless make-up immediately set them apart. "He wore the most outrageous clothes he could find," remembered Kevin of his brother, "and he wore face paint. That was because he really liked Kiss."

Wood took his assumption of stardom way too seriously. Like both his brothers, he soon fell into the chaos of drug dependence. Andy delved the deepest of the trio: he dabbled with junk when he was 18 in 1984, and was a known addict within a year. By 1986, when Malfunkshun's first recordings were on sale in Seattle, Wood had contracted the needle-user's nightmare, hepatitis. That summer, he was committed to a special hospital for a drug cure; but Wood never had the personality to conquer his chemical needs.

Most of the time, it didn't seem to matter. Wood christened himself L'Andrew The Love Child, carrying hippie philosophy into the devil's den. Besides fronting Malfunkshun, he doubled as an Elton John wanna-be, singing sensitive supper-club ballads with an air of melodrama borrowed from Judy Garland. Mostly, though, he was a glam poseur - an entirely self-conscious one.

Jonathan Poneman, whose Sub Pop label was acclaimed outside Seattle as the creator, or at

SOUNDGARDEN'S CHRIS CORNELL MEETS THE PEOPLE DURING THE LOLLAPALOOZA TOUR.

COBAIN'S STAGECRAFT WALKS A PERILOUS LINE BETWEEN PSYCHOTHERAPY AND PUNK CLICHE.

least the catalyst, of the local rock scene, put Wood and his band into perfect perspective: "In my mind, Andy Wood and Malfunkshun were the originators of the alleged Seattle sound - insofar as that sound is itself a parody, a send-up of all those Seventies bands and clichés. No-one was more totally into that, or more convincing, than Andy." So convincing was Wood, in fact, that when he billed himself as "the world's greatest rock'n'roll frontman", he believed every word.

If the Seattle sound was a parody, no-one told Soundgarden. The first of the 'alternative' Seattle bands to reach a national audience, they celebrated the Seventies that no-one in the underground cognoscenti was prepared to acknowledge - Alice Cooper, Kiss, Black Sabbath. Vocalist Chris Cornell had a passing fancy for the Meat Puppets; drummer Matt Cameron swore allegiance to the shades of Coltrane and Hendrix; Hiro Yamamoto (bass) admired the guerrilla tactics of The Butthole Surfers; guitarist Kim Thayil was raised on The MC5. But Soundgarden's music was never as exploratory as Coltrane, as satirical as The Butthole Surfers, or as political as The MC5. They were heavy, they were loud, and they were defiantly non-sexist; and in Chris Cornell they had the premier sex symbol of the Seattle scene. Cornell, cynics said, could afford to be a New Man.

In 1982, Hiro Yamamoto - the only member of Seattle's Asian population to make an impact on the local rock scene, possibly because he was actually born in Chicago - had a band called The Shemps. Chris Cornell became their vocalist; a week or two later, Hiro quit (nothing personal, I hope) and another ex-denizen of the Windy City, Kim Thayil, took his place. After Yamamoto, The Shemps' effective leader was guitarist Matt Dentino, who chose the band's repertoire of covers, to which only dead people (paging Jimi Hendrix, Buddy Holly and Jim Morrison) need apply.

Dentino was ousted by 1984, the year when Cornell started flatsharing with Yamamoto (there, I told you it was nothing personal). Retaining the services of guitarist Thayil, they formed Soundgarden - originally as a trio, with Cornell doubling on vocals and drums. Their name came from a bizarre sculpture in the city's Sand Point park - a sound sculpture, to be precise, comprised of steel tubes, arranged to catch the sounds of the wind, and create the eerie echo of the heavens. Soundgarden stole the idea, if not necessarily the noise, and recruited Scott Sundquist on drums to free Cornell as a vocalist. Finally, in 1986, Matt Cameron replaced Sundquist. His credentials were impeccable, as he'd played for years in Jack Endino's Skin Yard, and its predecessor Feedback; he'd even sung 'Puberty Love' in cult flick *Attack Of The Killer Tomatoes*.

All the while, Kim Thayil worked as a DJ at

KCMU, alongside Jonathan Poneman. "One afternoon," Jon wrote years later, "I received a message from the proprietor of a tavern called the Fabulous Rainbow. I was able to sleaze into the job of Tuesday Night booking czar. At the time, the local tavern rock scene was dominated by grabola R&B with an occasional serving of loopy new wave. Metal ruled the 'burbs to the east of Lake Washington. Most of the early bands who would later be associated with the embryonic 'Seattle sound' were still playing at Gorilla Gardens, an unsavory all-ages club." And at the Rainbow, Poneman first booked, and heard, Soundgarden. "They play soul music," he enthused to friends. "We were cool but people thought we were weird - a heavy art band, kind of punk," said Thayil confusingly.

Beyond the exterior facade of arrogance, there was a rare unity to the Seattle scene in 1985. "We talked about each other's bands, what we liked about them, what we hated," Chris Cornell remembered. "We talked a lot about music, and drank a lot." The public exhibition of this unity came late in 1985, with the release of 'Deep Six' - the first great Seattle compilation, and a primer for what eventually became known as grunge.

Alongside Green River, Malfunkshun, Soundgarden and The Melvins, 'Deep Six' featured Jack Endino's Skin Yard and The U-Men. Endino produced the record, at his suitably-named Reciprocal Studio in Seattle; by the end of the decade, he could rest on his laurels as the 'man who created grunge'. The LP came out on a local label (of course) called C/Z, which had been formed that year by Daniel House - a bandmate of Endino in Skin Yard, and an eternal enthusiast for the local music scene. Though House swears that 'Deep Six' will never be reissued - "Most of the bands on the record would be really pissed off at me, and embarrassed" - the album deserves to be exhumed, if only as an historical document. As another luminary of the local scene, Jonathan Poneman, put it: "It represented a lot of what was to blossom. You can hear that frenzied energy in its rawest state." Chris Cornell agrees: "When 'Deep Six' came out, we all said, 'Yeah, this is a way cooler scene than anywhere else'."

"Everyone was in their basements experimenting, and they were doing it with absolutely no idea in the world that anyone would notice, or care", remembered Dawn Anderson. 'Deep Six' gave the burgeoning Seattle underground some kind of internal cohesion; it erected a framework under which all the participating bands could shelter. But as yet, there were no waves reaching beyond Pugetopolis - except the freak tides that swept to Aberdeen, via The Melvins, or East to Ellensberg, where another group of would-be rock'n'roll stars, The Screaming Trees, were suffering similar isolation to Cobain and Novoselic.

One brand of Seattle music that was most definitely being heard outside Washington State was the pervasive, poisonous sound of the Muzak Corporation - or Yesco, as it was rather eerily named in the early Eighties. There worked a core of punk rockers, among whom was Tad Doyle: "It was a bit like going to school, more a case of messing about listening to tapes and stuff than doing any work. I met Bruce Pavitt there, along with Mark Arm and Chris Pugh, who formed Swallow. We listened to the loudest music possible when we were out of there - to wake us up and keep us alive."

Pavitt has already featured in this story, as a DJ at the punk-friendly KAOS station in Olympia. Born in 1959, in Park Forest, Illinois, he attended the same school as Soundgarden guitarist Kim Thayil. In his late teens, he made regular trips into downtown Chicago in search of the punk records he'd read about in the underground press - Television, Patti Smith, then later Dead Kennedys and Black Flag. Around 1979, he began a course at the extremely liberal Evergreen State College (along with cartoonist and creator of *The Simpsons*, Matt Groening).

Besides infiltrating the airwaves with his supply of punk singles, Pavitt also managed to introduce punk into the seminar-room. He extended his enthusiasm into a BA in Expressive Studies, in which he documented the significance of the independent labels on the growth of the alternative rock culture. Between times, he assembled an irregular fanzine, entitled *Subterranean Pop*, with each issue devoted to chronicling a regional music scene. It began as a subsidiary of John Foster's magazine *OP*, which itself mutated into *Option*, today America's most intelligent journal of underground musics. Issue 1, at the end of 1979, extended to just 200 copies; two issues and a year later, that print-run had been quadrupled, and after a setback with issue 4, Pavitt settled on distributing around 1,000 copies.

Issue 5 was a landmark: the magazine (its title now reduced to *Sub Pop*) came with a cassette compilation, which gathered together tracks by alternative bands from across the country. Pavitt himself contributed an ode called 'Debbie'; but aside from The Beakers, and Steve Fisk, whose track was a satirical soundbite collage called 'Reagan Speaks For Himself', the tape included no Seattle performers. Two further *Sub Pop* cassettes, in 1982 and 1983, came no closer to being the official voice of the Seattle scene.

In April 1983, Pavitt stepped a few yards closer to the mainstream, beginning a monthly column for the city's premier music paper, *The Rocket*. His *Sub Pop* pieces ran regularly for more than five years, effectively replacing the need for the fanzine.

The urge to compile hadn't deserted Pavitt,

however, who in July 1986 turned *Sub Pop* from a magazine column into a label, in time to issue 5,000 LPs and 500 cassettes of *Sub Pop 100*: a various artists collection that trawled in tracks by Scratch Acid, Sonic Youth and influential Oregon hard rockers, the Wipers, but again only two local acts, the U-Men and another ex-KAOS DJ, Steve Fisk.

Pavitt wasn't intent on ignoring the Seattle scene he'd been trying to boost during his radio days: in fact, he was already promising to issue an EP by Mark Arm's Green River. Even before their appearance on 'Deep Six', Green River had managed to sneak out a record on the New York-based indie label, Homestead. 'Come On Down' featured the new five-piece line-up of the band, with former Ducky Boys guitarist Stone Gossard joining Arm, Steve Turner, Alex Vincent and Jeff Ament for the sessions in December 1984. The EP came out the following summer, but was overshadowed by the simultaneous debut album by Dinosaur - later to become Dinosaur Jr.

On stage, Green River were often discordant and ragged: observers recall that the entire band tended to solo at once. Looking back, Mark Arm was quite content with their slow progress: "Not everyone's music is meant to be heard everywhere." And he noted the continued gulf between the band and their audience: "When we first started out, the crowd used to scream for us to play faster." But visually, the band had borrowed as much from Andrew Wood's Malfunkshun as from The New York Dolls: high cheekboned, scarves strategically placed around their necks and waists, they mixed sexual threat with an undercurrent of satire. New York hadn't objected to their image-mongering: the band were happy to be 'discovered' at CBGBs by ex-Aerosmith guitarist Joe Perry during an exploratory visit to New York, and delayed a follow-up to 'Come On Home' while Perry toyed with the idea of producing them.

Back in Seattle, it was the ubiquitous Jack Endino who produced their 'Dry As A Bone' EP in June 1986. The tapes were left to rot while Pavitt scurried to find the finance for a second Sub Pop release. Then Kim Thayil introduced him to someone he should already have known: Jonathan Poneman.

Born in 1960 and raised in Ohio, Poneman had graduated to the same college radio circuit as Bruce Pavitt, who must at the very least have heard Jon's Audioasis show on KCMU, where he was Programme Director. Poneman also played guitar in the Treeclimbers, and promoted punk shows at the Rainbow. There he saw Soundgarden perform for the first time, and resolved to help them issue a single, 'Hunted Down'.

Thayil's fortuitous intervention brought together Sub Pop's "corporate magnet", Pavitt, with "corporate lackey" Poneman. Jonathan

THE FAMILY COBAIN, CAUGHT IN THE MIDDLE OF THE 1992 MEDIA HURRICANE.

COURTNEY LOVE ENTERTAINS THE LA PATRONS AT JABBERJAW IN MARCH 1991.

provided the cash, Pavitt the enthusiasm and ideas: Pavitt seems to have been *de facto* 'leader' of the partnership, though Poneman was its self-appointed philosopher and spokesman. "We entered this not so much as business people but as fans," he admitted. C/Z boss Daniel House, quickly called in by Pavitt to help market Sub Pop releases, concurs: "I think Bruce Pavitt is a creative mastermind. I think Jonathan is a master of hype. But the one thing I don't believe either of them are, is businessmen."

Pavitt and Poneman spent $40,000 launching the Sub Pop label - around half of that a precarious bank loan. "We also went out of business in the first sixty days," Pavitt recalled. "It was only through a fluke - only because the jacket manufacturer in Canada decided to let us have the Green River covers before we had paid for them - that we stayed in business. That record took forever to come out - and it nearly killed us." This hand-to-mouth routine became more the norm than the exception over the next four years. But 'Hunted Down' and 'Dry As A Bone' reached the shops in June 1987; and a record on Sub Pop became a feasible goal for anyone in Seattle who could identify with Green River and Soundgarden's blend of metal, glam and punk.

Back in Aberdeen, Kurt Cobain hadn't even set his sights that high. "We never expected to get on Sub Pop," he explained in 1989, "we never even expected to put out a record. At the time we were recording our stuff, we didn't even know Sub Pop existed. When we recorded our first demo, we didn't realise they were a label. Even later when they'd put out the Soundgarden and Green River EPs, I didn't take much notice of that stuff. It wasn't like that was our premier goal."

Only seven years after the fact, the pre-history of Nirvana is shrouded in mystery. Some locals claim that the fledgling line-up of the band had only a handful of original songs; others that the core of the 'Bleach' album was in place as early as 1986. Then there's the demo tape that won the band a Sub Pop deal - was it credited to Skid Row, to Fecal Matter or to Nirvana? Every witness tells a different tale.

Whatever the exact details, Chris Novoselic's commitment to the band in 1986 seems to have been less than total. Though elsewhere he says he was working with Cobain as early as 1984, he recalls: "Kurt has this tape, which he made with Dale, the drummer of The Melvins. That was in 1986. I heard it, and thought it was really cool, so I said to start the band. And we started the band." Hearing the depth of Cobain's passion for his music obviously hardened Novoselic's interest: thereafter he was as central to the multi-named band as Kurt himself.

That first demo tape was recorded around September 1986, nine months before the Green

River and Soundgarden EPs reached the shops. As Chris said, it was a two-man collaboration between Cobain (guitar/bass/vocals) and Melvins percussionist Dale Crover, who maintained his band's reputation for generosity to other musicians. Cut on a four-track recorder lent by Kurt's aunt, who was doing her best to encourage her nephew at a time when he was estranged from both parents, it featured several of the songs from Nirvana's early Sub Pop releases. Most of them were Cobain compositions - passing snapshots of Aberdeen life, wrapped in enough local references and in-jokes to elude interpretation by outsiders. 'Floyd The Barber', 'Negative Creep' and 'Spank Thru' were all in existence by this stage, each one testament to their creator's fascination with the slow-motion punk of The Melvins.

That winter, Cobain and Novoselic made the fateful move to Seattle. A few months later, they and Dale Crover cut a ten-track demo tape with Jack Endino at Reciprocal. Though Cobain had registered that Endino had produced The Melvins' contributions to 'Deep Six', he was unaware that the Skin Yard guitarist was fast becoming the midwife of the Seattle underground - not to mention his band's own doom-rock, as showcased on their 1986 début album for C/Z. While Cobain and Novoselic recruited drummer Aaron Burkhart for live shows in Seattle's tiny rock clubs - venues like the Vogue and the Central, neither of which could hold more than 200 people - Jack Endino posted a copy of the tape to Jonathan Poneman. Intrigued by Kurt's "beautiful yet horrifying voice", Poneman called him, and set up a meeting in a downtown coffee shop.

The initial encounter was smoothed by Cobain's enthusiasm for Soundgarden, and his awareness that Poneman had been responsible for signing them up. Then Chris Novoselic arrived, determined not to be impressed, and began to throw in a few jibes to the effect that he wasn't overawed by any downtown company man with money in his pocket. Poneman lapped up this display of authentic punk attitude, and offered Nirvana - the name was finally settled - the chance to issue a Sub Pop single.

A week or two later, Bruce Pavitt met Kurt Cobain for the first time: "It was in 1987, at his apartment, which was loaded up with a lot of thrift-store knick-knacks, huge posters of Queen and The Rolling Stones, and little cages with pets everywhere. And I remember distinctly his pet rat bit me and I screamed quite loudly. I remember thinking he seemed kind of like a Eighties idea of a beatnik. The guy obviously wasn't spending a lot of hours at work, and was just kind of living on a thrift-store aesthetic."

Pavitt's view of Cobain as a working-class original is ironic, in view of Sub Pop's reputation for issuing records devoted to that same thrift-store aesthetic - Tad and Mudhoney spring

NIRVANA

NIRVANA
Nevermind

VERMIN

RVANA
LTH CLUB

OP
2
H
3

Hanako

OPEN

immediately to mind. In 1987, however, the label had yet to gain its 'lumberjack' image. Its prime exhibit that year was 'Screaming Life', a mini-LP by Soundgarden, cut on a tight budget of two thousand dollars. Confirming the band's in-built musical vision and strict adherence to the punk/Sabbath crossover, 'Screaming Life' had, in Poneman's words, "a devastating impact in music circles. From day one, Soundgarden was ballyhooed as the great saviours of rock'n'roll." The band began to feature in tentative press coverage of a 'Seattle sound', though there was more enthusiasm locally for Metal Church and especially Queensryche. Meanwhile, Tacoma bluesman Robert Cray had conformed to local tradition by finding success only after he'd left the state. "It had gotten so that no-one in Seattle could really take a local act seriously while they remained within the city limit," wrote fanzine editor Matt Black.

Outside Seattle, 1987 had been a year of change for the American rock underground. Byron Coley, editor of hardcore fanzine *Forced Exposure*, explained: "There's a lot of stuff that has been gestating for a while, but people just started to recognise it in 1987. Bands that you used to be able to go and see, and no-one would be there, their shows are completely filled with college students capering around. It's hard to pin down, though, because bands like The Butthole Surfers and Sonic Youth have been around for so long. Bands that people are recognising now, have really extensive and elaborate discographies by this time, which is different to what happened in the past. There's a large number of records coming out of America, too, wherever you go. When you go out to buy a record and see 200 new releases by bands you never heard of, I think it's a little daunting."

The hardcore explosion of 1982/83, which saw hundreds of American bands forming their own fly-by-night companies to issue two-minute rants about boredom or the price of beer, fractured the tight walls erected by the major-league labels. Purely because of its size, America has always been a difficult - impossible, some might say - market for indies to crack. Outside of local, self-generating scenes, and the ever-expanding college radio market, there is no place for the indies to expand. Distribution is nightmarish unless you can afford the punitive terms demanded by the majors. Even the most successful indie label in the States enjoys better coverage of its releases in Britain and Europe, for instance, than it does outside a handful of major American cities.

So the indie labels weren't about to overthrow Columbia, Capitol or Warner Brothers. But they could divert cash that might otherwise have been heading for Peter Frampton or The Eagles. Indie outlets could sustain themselves on a tiny fraction of the majors' break-even points: Sub

Pop, for example, limited themselves to a few thousand copies of all their early releases, and still hoped to make a profit. On a major, you could sell 200,000 albums and get dropped six months later as a loss-maker.

There were other advantages to indie-dom. Major labels depended for their sales on mass-markets - anything from Woolworth's to supermarts - which wouldn't be prepared to stock (or expect to sell) underground music. Likewise, their chart positions depended on Top 40 airplay, and even the most successful alternative rock rarely breaks into that advertising-heavy format. Top 40 depends on smooth, comfortable listening; anyone who challenges listener prejudices is automatically a pariah.

But there were signs that sectors of the mainstream were prepared to toy with the margins. Hüsker Dü began life in Minneapolis as a hardcore outfit around 1980, and grew to become one of the few bands to develop punk into intelligent, questioning rock music without sweetening their sound. They signed to Warners in 1986, and split a couple of years later; but only after selling enough records to convince the majors that punks could be marketed with kid gloves.

Elsewhere, bands like The Butthole Surfers and Sonic Youth had moved beyond hardcore into a genre that defied description. The Buttholes gradually extended their culture-sniping until they became a cornucopia of U.S. low-life, a shopper's guide to the dark side of the American dream. Sonic Youth came out of the No Wave scene that succeeded New York punk: part art, part punk, they toyed with the simplest of song structures, rowdying their way through a two-chord, snotty-nosed primal rant and then sabotaging the entire exercise with a sudden burst for the borders of common sense and decency. Often self-indulgent but never predictable, Sonic Youth claimed punk as their heritage and the avant-garde as their territory. They rocked out hard enough to please college audiences, but retained enough edge for the underground. And they used their rapidly increasing clout in the industry as talent scouts, effecting a series of vital introductions that transformed the face of alternative rock over the next five years.

Like Hüsker Dü and Black Flag, Sonic Youth had played regular Seattle shows in the mid-Eighties, usually insisting on Green River as their support act, and their influence began to rub off on the locals. In effect, they were putting into practice what Jonathan Poneman proposed as the Sub Pop ethic: "Punk rock in the States basically started as a conceptual movement. Bruce and I have very consciously tried to fuse those concepts with the more populist end of hardcore." Listen to Sonic Youth's 'Sister' or 'Evol', and any further explanations are unnecessary.

45

The gradual twisting of hardcore away from its ragged skeleton also stripped away its emotional impact. What began as a simple statement of emotion, be it boredom, anger or despair, gradually became something more consciously artistic - less felt than imagined. And for the moment, that wasn't something that interested Kurt Cobain, at least when it came to his own work. "All my early songs were really angry," he declared in 1989, which was another way of confirming that they were all about his past.

It's ironic, then, that Nirvana's first record came out of love, not anger. Not only was its title 'Love Buzz', but it was a longtime favourite of Kurt's, from his early childhood, when he'd first heard the original version of the song by Dutch pop band Shocking Blue. "It seems so commercial now," Cobain noted in April 1989, but the pop fizz was defiantly removed from the song, and replaced by a pulsing bass riff, some metallic guitar, and a squall of feedback where they might have been a solo.

Cut at the same early 1988 session - with Jack Endino, naturally - was 'Big Cheese'. The drumming, by new Nirvana member Chad Channing, powered this wry look at authority and obedience, slung together without a moment's care for narrative development. Also unveiled during this session was 'Hairspray Queen', which remained unreleased for nearly five years - by which time it somehow reminded Kurt Cobain "how incredibly New Wave we were", a strange way of describing a vicious blend of instrumental power and vocal incoherence that owed a lot to Scratch Acid.

Pavitt and Poneman elected to issue 'Love Buzz' and 'Big Cheese' as a single, but not before the customary delay - it didn't reach the shops until October 1988, and then only in a limited run of 1,000 copies. The exclusivity was quite deliberate: Sub Pop used the record to inaugurate their Singles Club, whereby members would pay $35 a year for the privilege of receiving regular 45s unavailable elsewhere.

Such marketing devices were not only a neat way of improving the label's cash flow. They also heightened the public acceptance of Sub Pop as an elite, heightened by T-shirts like the one which proudly proclaimed 'Loser' at the height of the media obsession with yuppies. Jon Poneman was all too aware of the potential power of bucking the official mood of the country - and equally certain that government optimism wasn't shared by those outside the country's most prosperous centres. By cutting back on welfare payments and services, sharpening the rods of media censorship, and engaging in futile military jaunts overseas, the Reagan administration had effectively disenfranchised a whole generation of thinking American youth. Poneman was both appalled and strangely heartened: "The past eight years," he said in 1988, "have created an environment

in this country where what we are doing is actually a viable form of rebellion. It's a liberating factor. It's amazing that this stuff can still rile people. We like the idea that we can get a reaction." And Tad Doyle, shortly to become a Sub Pop artist himself, noted that the label was "a big middle finger to the corporate world".

Not that Sub Pop didn't have corporate ideas of its own. Bruce Pavitt: "When we started out, we recognised that pop music, as part of the culture, was more than just a guitar riff. There's a visual sensibility, a production sound. So we got Charles Peterson, who had been documenting the scene from the beginning, to be our photographer. And Jack Endino, a great producer with a very distinctive sound, has worked on most of our stuff."

Label, photographer and producer combined to greatest effect on the epochal 'Sub Pop 200' compilation - the first record on the label to attract interest overseas, and still the most accurate document of the original Seattle sound after 'Deep Six'. Marketing again: the set was packaged as three 12" EPs, complete with a 20-page booklet of Charles Peterson's photos, which established running sweat and lank, flowing hair as the visual image of Sub Pop. "It wasn't like somebody said, 'Let's all dress like lumberjacks and start Seattle chic'," said Poneman, but they might as well have done. And to tie the entire Seattle package together, someone - it was probably Poneman - came up with the generic title of 'grunge'. "It could have been sludge, grime, crud, any word like that," he explained later. But grunge it was.

Nirvana's contribution to the set was the strangely uncharacteristic 'Spank Thru', which started out like an R.E.M. demo before lapsing into the familiar grunge. Local reviewers ignored the track in favour of more aggressive offerings by Tad, Mudhoney and Soundgarden, but Nirvana did pick up their first review in *The Rocket*, when Grant Alden presciently described 'Love Buzz' as "too clean for thrash, too pure for metal, too good to ignore".

The media blitz for 'Sub Pop 200' delayed the release of he band's début album, 'Bleach'. "We recorded it in three days," Novoselic remembered, "hacked it in, hacked it out", and the entire recording costs (not including the final mixdown) came to a ridiculous $606.17 - which wouldn't cover a day's food in the studio for a major label band.

"The album is similar to the single in song material," Kurt Cobain reckoned, "but we've recorded it a lot rawer. It sounds better - harder." And so it did. For anyone first entranced by the punk-pop of 'Nevermind', 'Bleach' might sound oppressively stark and bare. Songs begin with the most basic of bass or drum patterns, before Cobain's guitar lumbers into action, and the band thrash their way through a repeated riff, with howling, indecipherable vocals.

KURT COBAIN UNPLUGGED DURING A TOWER RECORDS IN-STORE SHOWCASE.

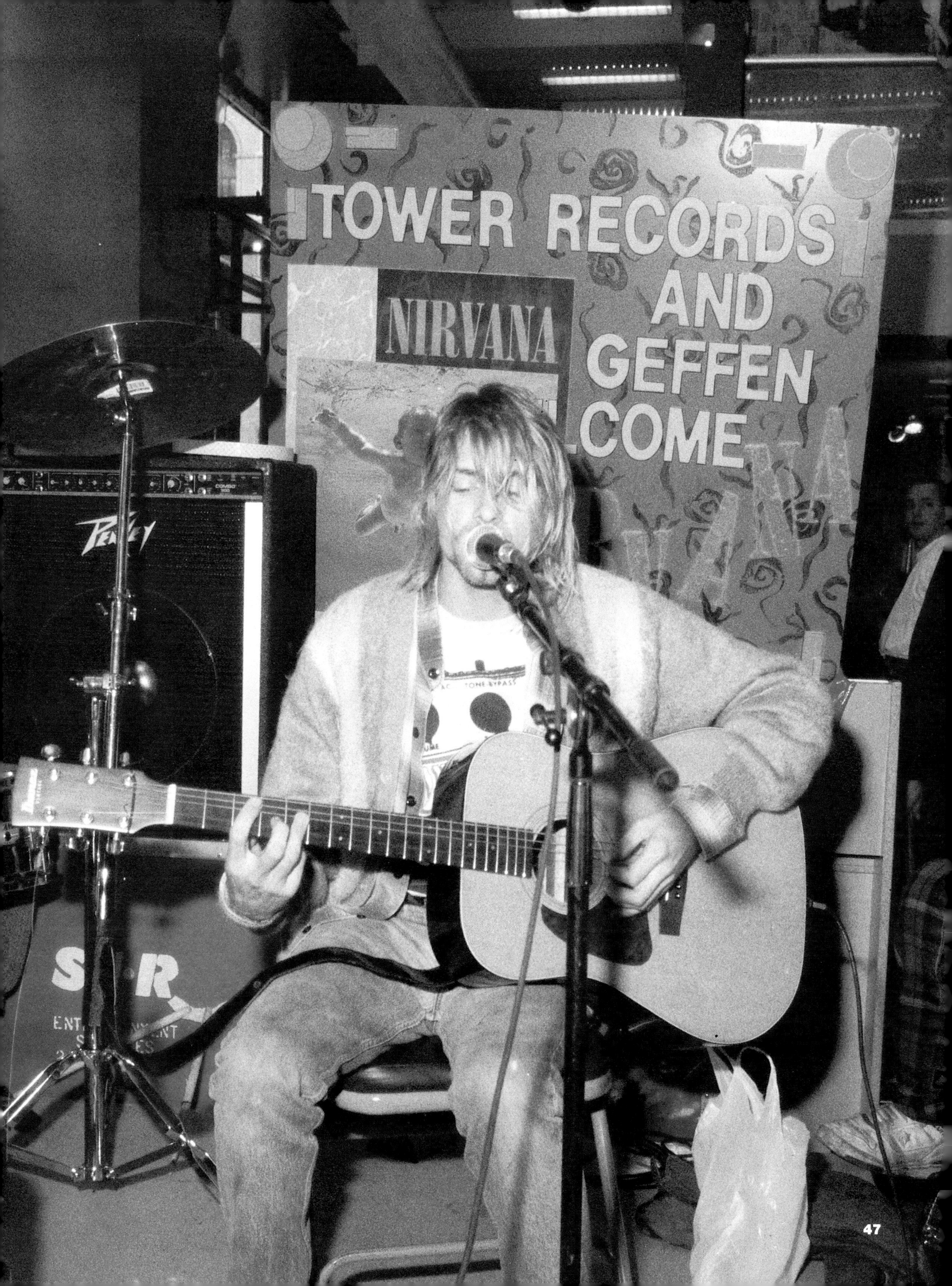
TOWER RECORDS
AND
GEFFEN
LCOME
NIRVANA

CHRIS NOVOSELIC, NIRVANA BASSIST AND CROATIA'S MOST PROMINENT
AND POLITICALLY ASTUTE CONTRIBUTION TO ROCK'N'ROLL.

52

Approach the album from the other direction, and its thrust is easy to understand. Nirvana had been listening to Sabbath, to Scratch Acid, to Sonic Youth and to Steve Albini's Big Black - where thudding drumbeats laid down an unmoving bedrock for savage explorations of angst and desire. The Big Black influence is most apparent on 'Sifting' - though Cobain dissolved the noise briefly with a beautifully placed pop chorus - while the joys of repetition fired songs like 'Negative Creep' (with its eerie hookline, "Johnny's little girl ain't a girl no more") and 'Scoff'.

Two tracks on the album dated back to the Cobain/Novoselic/Crover sessions of early 1987 - and The Melvins' blueprint was instantly audible on the sluggish 'Paper Cuts', topped with a Lennon-esque scream that proved Kurt hadn't forgotten his Beatles records. Their pop melodies were most obvious on 'About A Girl', which could be a dry run for the 'Nevermind' album. Mostly, though, 'Bleach' was a hard rock album; and its lyrics remained strictly personal, simply because they were buried indecipherably in the mix. "We were afraid to play pop music because we felt that people wouldn't accept it," Cobain admitted a couple of years later.

There were six or seven leftovers that didn't make the album - not just 'Spank Thru', but also curiosities like 'Aero Zeppelin' ("Christ!," wrote Cobain in 1992. "Yeah, let's just throw together some heavy metal riffs in no particular order and give it a quirky name in homage to a couple of our favourite masturbatory Seventies rock acts."), 'Beeswax' and 'Mexican Seafood'. Some made ideal giveaways when friends came calling with compilations on their mind; others remained hidden until rounded up on 'Incesticide' in December 1992. None of them would have improved the album, or quickened the arrival of Nirvana-mania. In 1988, Cobain, Novoselic and Chad Channing were unashamedly a grunge band: pop stardom would have to wait.

When the first copies of 'Sub Pop 200' reached Britain before Christmas 1988, one fell into the hands of the country's most influential underground DJ, John Peel, who plugged it heavily in his column in *The Observer*, and on his late-night BBC radio show. Deeply impressed, and aware that there was now a potential market for their products overseas, Poneman and Pavitt hit upon an ingenious marketing scheme. "The very idea that we would pay to fly in a journalist from Great Britain, after *they* had solicited *us*, to do those articles," exclaimed Poneman a year later, still overawed by his own idea. The journalist was Everett True, from *Melody Maker* in London; the articles were a series of Sub Pop profiles and puffs which created an immediate demand for live performances by the label's top bands, and cemented Sub Pop's place as the most daring

and intuitive indie label in America.

'Sub Pop 200' had created the stir: when True rang Pavitt and Poneman to get the story, they volunteered to pay his way. The result was a major feature on their label, which raved: "Sub Pop is the lifeforce to the most vibrant, kicking scene encompassed in one city for at least ten years". That quote alone paid back the airfare.

Ironically, *Melody Maker* wasn't the British paper which had been offering the most coverage of Seattle bands prior to the appearance of the '200' collection. Nor did that honour fall to the *NME*, still priding itself as being the most farsighted of what were then the three major UK rock weeklies. Instead, it was *Sounds* who got the scoop, profiling Soundgarden regularly through 1987 and 1988, and also dipping into Screaming Trees and Beat Happening as well.

At that point, there was no rivalry, because Seattle seemed like an ideal *Sounds* story. The background of the three papers was essential knowledge before you could pick up all the nuances. During the British pop explosion of the 60s, it was *NME* which ruled the roost, far outselling its b&w tabloid rivals. Rooted entirely around the Top 30 singles chart, it became the indispensable journal of record, treated as the Bible by both fans and insiders. But it proved unable to cope with the rock/pop split after 1967, concentrating on lightweight chart acts while the previously jazz-centred *Melody Maker* came into its own, and ran long, provocative and intelligent interviews with the most talented of the rock newcomers.

When *Sounds* was launched in early1970, staffed mostly by ex-*MM* writers and aimed directly at the 'progressive'/post-teen rock market, the other papers had to react, or die. *Melody Maker* would strip away its folk, jazz and blues coverage as the decade progressed but for a couple of years during 1971/72 it led the pack by a country mile, occasionally selling over 200,000 issues a week, an all time record for a UK weekly music magazine; *NME* dithered for a year or two before belatedly heading leftwards itself. It gathered in writers from London's leading underground papers, and reinvented itself as a bastion of hipness - Britain's most turned-on rock mag.

The trouble was, both *NME* and *Melody Maker* missed punk. *Sounds* kept feelers closer to the ground than its competitors, and had six or nine months to itself, championing the Pistols, The Clash and The Damned, before *NME* and (very reluctantly) *Melody Maker* followed suit. As usual, *NME* pretended it had discovered everything itself, and its coverage of what happened next was, true to form, more insightful than the others'. But *Sounds* had shown a knack for catching rock movements at their inception, even if they could never quite make them their own.

They put that right at the end of the 70s,

creating the montrosity that was Oi!. While *Sounds* lauded the frequently right-wing antics of the skinheads to the skies, *NME* and *Melody Maker* treated the entire episode with contempt. *NME* was deep into a left-wing political stance that was succeeded in the early Eighties by a bizarre flirtation with philosophical concepts like structuralism and semiotics; *Melody Maker* kept its eye on the mainstream, but always smelled slightly stale.

By the mid-Eighties, *NME* had rejected elitist writing about 'culture' in favour of a search for a new punk - where anything from The Pogues to the Jesus & Mary Chain could qualify. *Sounds* was a ghetto for heavy metal, hard rock and (ironically enough) hardcore - hence the interest in Soundgarden and their ilk. And *Melody Maker* took a brave, if possibly suicidal, leap towards its own brand of philosophical moderism. By 1989, the paper exuded passion - a healthy, if sometimes overwhelming, alternative to *NME*'s mix of political enthusiasm and musical cynicism. Selected artists were treated to orgasmic reviews that transformed their music into a psychic force wielding the power of life and death; sometimes the emotional weight grew too much, and the writers (each uniquely personal) lapsed into incoherent verbal weeping.

So Sub Pop's choice of paper - and, as it turned out, writer - could hardly have been better. *NME* waited a few months, and then slowly began to examine Seattle itself; saddest of all, *Sounds* continued to chronicle all things hardcore until its publishers went into liquidation in 1991, just before Nirvana broke out. Had it survived until 'Nevermind', everything might have been different: at the very least, it would have had the satisfaction of revealing that it had beaten the others to the punch, for the second decade running.

The European fame rebounded to Seattle, where the simple fact that a local band had made the cover of *Melody Maker* was a front-page story in itself. The even more simple fact that few people in Seattle had ever heard of Mudhoney was even more revealing. It confirmed that for all its attention to the media, Sub Pop was a long way from becoming the mainstream music of Seattle. When Washington State journalists picked their tips for the top, only Soundgarden from the Sub Pop community (who had already set sail for major-label waters, via A&M) won any votes. And no-one so much as mentioned Nirvana in the local rock press beyond the occasional review, and the addition of their name to the label roster in their infrequent stories on Sub Pop.

While Nirvana waited for 'Bleach' to be released, the attention that could have been theirs was focused on Mudhoney. Sub Pop kept issuing new singles, by Swallow, Blood Circus, and their first out-of-town act, The Fluid from

MUDHONEY, COLLEGE GRADUATES
MASQUERADING AS LOW-LIFE DEVILS
OF EXCESS.

THE FREEWHEELIN' MARK ARM,
VETERAN OF SEVERAL EARLY 1980'S
SEATTLE PUNK COMBOS.

"THE MORE PEOPLE ARE SCREAMING AT YOU, THE MORE YOU ARE INTO SMASHING EVERYTHING UP."

Denver. But it was the quartet Poneman christened "the masters of disease and grunge - loud ballads of love and dirt - the current masters of punk rock" who stole the stories in the media, first in Britain, then back in the States.

It wasn't surprising: they had their act fully rehearsed. Caricature is easier to assimilate than reality, and what Mudhoney offered was caricature brought to life. They peddled a strictly-for-laughs cartoon impression of rural North-West America, crossed with some splatter movie; and the British press lapped it up. They had punk credibility: Mark Arm and Steve Turner had quit Green River when the rest of the band wanted to sign a major-label deal. They had pedigree: aside from that pair, they boasted Matt Lukin from The Melvins on bass, Dan Peters from Bundle Of Hiss on drums. Their name - a perfect touch, this - was taken from a Russ Meyer movie, about the joys of illegal sex in a seedy Southern town. They worshipped garage rock, Iggy Pop and cult Brit-rocker Billy Childish. They took nothing seriously, least of all interviews. And Steve Turner and Mark Arm were moonlighting in a mock-punk band, The Thrown-Ups. Arm wrote their lyrics ("all I do is rhyme, man"); Turner added the music ("Notes and chords mean nothing to me. It's the attitude that counts."). What could have been better?

Plus they had the songs. Their debut single was 'Touch Me I'm Sick', a gruesome punk anthem which more than matched 'Anarchy In The UK' or Richard Hell's 'Blank Generation'. Mark Arm screeched like a torture victim, the guitars riffed like The Stooges on speed, and the entire spectacle was unforgettable. When they followed through four months later with a brilliant mini-album, 'Superfuzz Bigmuff' (dig those effects pedal references), they had the punk world at their feet.

"I had this sound in my head which was a lot louder and noisier than anything I'd ever heard," Mark Arm remembered about his early teens, "and Mudhoney is the closest anyone has yet come to that sound." They drew comparisons with The Sonics, and with Sonic Youth - who joined them on a split single, covering 'Touch Me I'm Sick' rather lazily while Mudhoney did their best with 'Halloween'. More to the point was their 'Hate The Police' EP, led off by their thrilling cover of a punk song by The Dicks.

March 1989 found them in the UK, supporting Sonic Youth, who were quick to add their imprimatur. In May, they were back in Britain, encouraging their student audiences to storm the stage, and winning reviews that greeted them as the return of punk-rock.

Mindful that Soundgarden had already tasted the bullet, they scoffed at suggestions they might sell out to a major label. "We're not a major label band," boasted Mark Arm. "And we wouldn't want to be," added Steve Turner. Arm finished the rumour off in style: "No-one's ever

talked to us from a major label. We pretty much told everybody that if they came around, we would just tell them to fuck off."

October 1989 brought a full-length album - which revealed nothing that they hadn't already shown, but then that was all you'd expect from cartoon characters (unless they're Matt Groening's). And before Christmas they were in Britain one more time, headlining the Sub Pop Lamefest UK over Tad and some Aberdeen band called Nirvana.

Only then, a year into their publicity hype, did they start to reveal some secrets. For a start, Turner and Arm weren't the all-American rural maniacs, high on inbreeding and drugs, that they'd been portraying all year. Turner announced that the band would have to be put on hold while he finished his degree - in Anthropology, no less (must have come in handy when he was swotting up on psychopaths). And Mark Arm was a graduate in English Literature, it transpired, addicted to the works of William Faulkner. If Iggy Pop had turned out to be a professor of history at Yale, the comedown couldn't have been harder.

Sub Pop's second-string most-likely-axe-maniac-to-win-a-Grammy nominee was Tad Doyle - a mountain of a man, a Seattle Gargantua or, as hecklers at an early London show put it rather unkindly, "you fat bastard". The hype this time was that Mr Tad was a lumberjack, with a chainsaw revved up behind every amp and a sick mind desperate to be satisfied. "Tad is a guy who likes to have fun and doesn't care what other people think," announced his record company, He had a band as well, conveniently called Tad, of whom only bassist Kurt Danielson ever raised his top-lip in public.

Taking the percussive thrust of Big Black, the grunge of Mudhoney and the preoccupations of American trash culture, Tad had it made. Their début album, 'God's Balls', was titled after a climactic moment in a cheap porn film. It included 'Sex God Missy', a terrifying tale of sexual hatred heard beneath the inane chatter of a CB radio, and 'Nipple Belt', which caught a Seattle preoccupation (Ted Bundy did his stuff in the town, don't forget) by picking up on a particularly unpleasant habit of Ed Gein and his Texas chainsaw massacre. "Just put it on the turntable and it saws away," read the press adverts.

'God's Balls' was certainly a powerful record, with hints of funk blurred into its primal rock thrust. So too was the 'tween-albums single 'Wood Goblins', plugged as "sick punk rock". And the second LP, 'Salt Lick', roared out of the speakers harder and louder than any Sub Pop record had ever done. 'Glue Machine' and 'High On The Hog' were the sound of the apocalypse reaching the Pacific North-West, and the North-West won.

Tad produced good copy too, whether the tales were apocryphal - like the time he was supposed to have relieved his bowels on stage in Leeds - or all too true, as when he grew the fearsome beard that gave him the aura of a 300-pound Charles Manson. Then, in July 1990, he announced he was cutting his third album with Butch Vig, and that "the new material will be a shock for many people". So it proved, as '8-Way Santa' was greeted as a pale shadow of excess by the British press. Worse still, its US release was stymied by a packaging disaster. No, Tad didn't chainsaw the mailman: rather, the sweet young married couple pictured in the cover photo, which Jon Poneman had picked up at a garage sale, didn't want their faces on the album. Why? Well, he was stripped to the waist; she was only wearing a bra; he was clutching her breast; and they'd since become born-again Christians. The album was hastily repackaged (Poneman doing his best to make a PR coup out of the story) but the sales momentum was lost, and the poor figures came close to sinking Sub Pop in the spring of 1991.

Worse still, as far as his image was concerned, Tad Doyle revealed he had a past. Being born in Boise, Idaho, was bearable; past membership of a punk rock band called H Hour was no problem at all. But spending his teenage years in a jazz quartet who entertained President Nixon at the White House, and then studying music theory in college? Get out of here.

At the two Lamefest shows (billed as "Seattle's lamest bands in a one-night orgy of sweat and insanity") - Seattle in June 1989, London that December - Mudhoney and Tad had been supported by Nirvana. By June, the band was a four-piece: to relieve Kurt Cobain from the awesome responsibility of playing lead and rhythm guitar and singing as well, Jason Everman had joined on second guitar in April. "We met him," explained Chris Novoselic, "and he seemed real nice. And he lent us the $600 to pay for the album to be made. We wanted to get another guitar player to thicken out the sound."

Everman scarcely survived three months. He got his picture on the cover of 'Bleach', and his name on the sleeve ("We still owe him the $600," Cobain smirked after he'd left, "maybe I should send him off a cheque"), though he hadn't played a note on the record. It was the touring which finished him, however. "It seemed like we just got more metal sounding," Kurt complained.

"Then we went on tour," Chris added, "and we just couldn't communicate with him anymore. He was just gone all the time."

"He'd get kind of pissed off, because that was when we went through a stage when we were smashing stuff up all the time, and he didn't like that," Cobain confirmed.

The split was eventually described as "a very

mutual decision", blamed on "artistic differences". Everman subsequently joined Soundgarden, and was kicked out again after a couple of months; "he just didn't work out" was the repeated chorus. Through it all, he maintained a dignified silence in response to Nirvana's jibes. All he would venture on his brief liaison with the band was a restrained "Touring is stressful, especially in a little tiny van out in the middle of Houston, in the middle of summer, touring around in a little mobile oven."

Instrument trashing was becoming a staple part of the average Nirvana show, which raised financial and artistic problems. "It's a nice feeling," Chris Novoselic insisted. "It needs to be done at least twice a week. It seems to be becoming more common at our gigs. The more people are screaming at you, the more you are into smashing everything up. It's definitely not a contrived thing. We don't smash the gear up on purpose, we're not trying to impress or anything."

But close observers began to wonder. At the Seattle Moore Festival, local rock journalist Gillian Gaar noticed that Cobain spent much of the show "writhing on the floor at the drop of a hat". A month later, they were sharing the bill with Tad at Maxwell's, a tiny club in Hoboken, New Jersey, as part of the New York New Music Seminar. The four-piece Nirvana entered lovingly into an auto-destruct fest at the end of their set, but it was still Tad who won the rave reviews.

On tour in Britain with Tad that October, reviewers noticed that the three-piece unit were markedly less powerful and organised onstage than the four-piece who'd visited in June. The band might have been wearing T-shirts describing them as "Fudge packing, crack smoking, satan worshipping, mother fuckers", but their performances were far less slick than that. In Rome, Kurt Cobain came close to the edge, as Bruce Pavitt told *Rolling Stone*: "After four or five songs, he quit playing and climbed up the speaker column and he was going to jump off. The bouncers were freaking out and everybody was just begging him to come down. And he was saying, 'No, No, I'm just going to dive'. He had really reached his limit. People saw a guy wig out in front of them, who could break his neck if he didn't get it together."

Kurt's 'wig out' ironically coincided with a period when he was claiming peace of mind as a recent addition to his life. "As time goes on," he admitted in October 1989, "my songs are getting poppier and poppier as I get happier and happier. The songs are now about conflicts in relationships, emotional things with other human beings. We're writing a lot more pop songs, like 'About A Girl' on 'Bleach'. Some people might think of that as 'changing' into something, but it's something we've always been aware of and are just now starting to express."

The follow-up to 'Bleach' was now scheduled for April 1990, though there was nothing on tape. As an experiment, Nirvana had cut a couple of songs in the summer of 1989 with Steve Fisk instead of Jack Endino, but neither 'Been A Son' nor 'Stain' matched Cobain's initial concept. 'Been A Son', with its oblique lyrics about sexual identity, did at least reflect Kurt's passion for writing pop songs; and the new material that evolved over the next three or four months confirmed that direction.

One of them was 'Polly', which Chris Novoselic confirmed was based on a newspaper story: "It's about a young girl who was abducted. The guy drove her around in his van. Tortured her. Raped her. The only chance she had of getting away was to come on to him and persuade him to untie her. That's what she did, and she got away. Can you imagine how much strength that took?" The facts were dramatic enough, but Cobain cranked the tension a couple of notches by setting the song in the mind of the abductor, so that it captures the girl's terror as filtered through his own confusion. And the prettiness of the tune shovelled another layer of irony over the proceedings.

"When I write a song," Cobain admitted in October 1989, "the lyrics are the least important thing. I can go through two or three different subjects in a song, and the title can mean absolutely nothing at all." That doesn't make Cobain's writing random, though, and it's hard to believe that there wasn't a degree of wit involved in christening one of the new songs 'Lithium' - the softest metal known to mankind. And the lyric, though not exactly a linear narrative, caught the confusion of teenage America - its sudden lurches from indifference to violence - perfectly, especially when allied to another miraculous pop melody. The closer Cobain came to unveiling his own indeterminacy in song, the more he claimed that the entire process was accidental. At this point, Kurt wasn't prepared to be his own spokesman, let alone anyone else's.

The song that impressed the Sub Pop crew was 'In Bloom', which had hit single written across every chorus, and seemed to accept the inevitable in its post-stardom lyrics. The label had taken to hyping the band's music thus: "Hypnotic and righteous heaviness from these Olympia pop stars. They're young, they own their own van, and they're going to make us rich!" 'In Bloom', 'Lithium', 'Polly' and the rest suggested they might be right.

Reflected glory from the British press finally attracted some major-label interest in the summer of 1989. As the premier PR men of the Seattle scene, it was Bruce Pavitt and Jon Poneman on whom the attention was focused. They'd taken to giving hyperbolic interviews, boosting their own importance, albeit tongue in cheek. "We're starmakers," Poneman told one local journalist, only for Pavitt to counter, "We

THE RED HOT CHILI PEPPERS, WHOSE FUNK DRIVEN HARD CORE ROCK PREPARED THE WAY FOR THE SEATTLE EXPLOSION.

invented the scene." Poneman topped him: "We ARE the scene." It was left to Pavitt to puncture the balloon: "And we could sell out, no problem."

For the moment, they refused to countenance the idea. Like Mudhoney, they dangled their independence like a talisman. But by July 1989, the offers were too frequent to ignore. Island Records snooped around the city, had meetings with Sub Pop, but never quite laid their cards on the table. "Island is a fine label with a great history," Jon Poneman agreed, "but they would never make a concrete proposal to us. They were enthusiastic on the artistic side, but their business people wouldn't let them pull the trigger."

The reluctance of Island's accountants to empty their coffers was understandable. Despite the press hype, and the trans-European reputation of their bands, Sub Pop's actual receipts were minimal. By the summer of 1989, the label had still not sold 10,000 copies of any individual release in the States. Mudhoney's 'Superfuzz Bigmuff' LP had reached 12,000, but that included sales from Europe. The rest was less impressive - 3,000 copies of Green River's 'Rehab Doll', 4,000 apiece of Mudhoney's 'Touch Me I'm Sick' and Soundgarden's 'Screaming Life'. Sit that alongside one million-plus for Queensryche's latest album, or the 500,000 sales of Metal Church's 'Blessing In Disguise', and it was easy to see why the money-men were less taken with Sub Pop's business deals than the A&R guys were with the press cuttings.

To put Sub Pop's sales into some kind of perspective, the summer of 1989 was when Mother Love Bone issued their debut EP, 'Shine'. Given distribution by Mercury, though actually released by the group's own Stardog label, the EP notched up 20,000 sales in a matter of months.

That must have been particularly galling for Mudhoney, as Mother Love Bone was the other half of Green River - the half that refused to ride the indie route - plus Andrew Wood, the charismatic frontman from the earliest of the Seattle grunge bands, Malfunkshun.

"Green River", said Bruce Pavitt in a moment of characteristic understatement, "destroyed the morals of a generation." That aim achieved, they destroyed their own, whatever they were. In July 1987, they began work on their first full-length album with - of course - Jack Endino, at Reciprocal Recording. They loosened up with a faithful rendition of Bowie's tribute to Lou Reed, 'Queen Bitch', and cut raw demos of raw songs like 'Porkfist' and 'Rehab Doll'. Their attitude was evidently intact.

For once, Endino didn't make the final cut. In August, the location switched to the 24-track studio of Steve Lawson Productions, where Bruce Calder seized Endino's role. It took five months to finish the album, but not much of that was spent in the studio. By the time that the final guitar overdubs were laid down in January 1988, Green River had already disintegrated.

The problem was ethical rather than aesthetic, and had a history that stretched back to 1986. Watching Soundgarden waltz onto a major label, bassist Jeff Ament craved similar recognition. Mark Arm toed the line of independence equalling authenticity. The battle simmered into the summer of 1987, when Ament took a showcase performance at the Scream Club in Los Angeles as an opportunity to invite a shoal of semi-interested A&R men to see Green River in action. Arm wanted backstage passes for his friends, only to discover that Ament had already exhausted the band's supply. When the promised A&R men didn't bother to cross town and catch the band's show, Arm announced he was through. "It was punk versus major-label deal," he explained a year later, and for the moment major-deal deal meant the death of ideals.

Bruce Fairweather, who'd replaced Steve Turner after an earlier crisis of principles, and Stone Gossard sided with Ament. Alex Vincent didn't jump either way, but simply fell out of contention, and ended up working in a local movie house. Green River split, leaving Ament and Gossard to supervise the final mixes of what became the 'Rehab Doll' album.

A month after the sessions finally closed, Arm and Turner were founding Mudhoney, while Ament and Gossard had elected to relocate to the satanic city of LA. Instead, they shared a few beers with Andrew Wood, dissatisfied that his drive for stardom hadn't brought him fame beyond purchasers of 'Deep Six' and the 200 or so patrons who could squeeze into Malfunkshun's Seattle club gigs.

By March 1988, Mother Love Bone were already rehearsing - Gossard, Wood, Ament and Fairweather having recruited drummer Greg Gilmore from Ten Minute Warning, a band whose other moment in rock legend consists of having provided Duff McKagen for Guns 'N Roses. "What we discovered in Mother Love Bone was how to take it easy," Stone Gossard volunteered, "letting things happen naturally and really jamming on stuff a lot more." With the jamming came a Seventies aesthetic which signalled the gradual diminution of the band's adherence to punk values. Talking late in 1988, Gossard listed his spiritual ancestors as Jimmy Page, Aerosmith and Elton John, which must have thrilled Mark Arm. In place of the trash obsession and neo-hardcore aggression of Green River, Mother Love Bone substituted a sense of pace and dynamics that had been learned from Seventies avatars like Led Zeppelin and Free.

Drawing on Andy Wood's case of unfinished poems, Mother Love Bone quickly prepared a demo tape, shipped out to agencies in Los Angeles in the hope of landing Californian gigs.

One copy reached Slash Records, the semi-indie who'd stepped neatly along the borders of punk for years, and prompted them to express an interest. Anna Statman was their A&R rep; by the time she contacted the band, she'd switched companies to Geffen. Statman introduced them to Seattle manager Kelly Curtis; and also arranged for Geffen to advance $5,000 to cut a more professional demo tape, which they did at Lawson Studios in June 1988. Both sides assumed a deal was simply a matter of time. But the stir of activity had awoken the A&R staff of other Hollywood labels.

"Suddenly people were flying up here to take the band to dinner," Kelly Curtis remembers, "people who had no idea, no clue as to what the band was about. I think part of what attracted all the attention was that it was something that was not happening anywhere else. Mother Love Bone was in a sense leading the scene. They were the best of what once was. They had the funk edge, the punk edge and the hard rock edge - they really did get better every time they played."

In July 1988, the band were telling everyone in Seattle about their Geffen contract. But that month, the perennial convulsions that afflict major record companies intervened, and Tom Zutaut (who'd already brought Guns 'N Roses to Geffen) took over Anna Statman's role in the negotiations. He took a while to find his feet, and in the interregnum Polygram crept in with an equally attractive offer. On November 19, Mother Love Bone signed a $250,000 deal, linking them to Polygram for seven albums; besides Geffen, four other major labels had their advances rejected. An anonymous Geffen spokesperson lashed out at the band: "Their britches became too large for their body very quickly. They tried to get as many labels, as many booking agents, as many scumbag parasitic people as there are in this business, to be as interested in this band as possible, and they blew the whole thing out of proportion."

Geffen's bitterness was heightened by the knowledge they'd chewed sour Seattle fruit once before. Before Mother Love Bone escaped their grasp, Soundgarden had also seemed likely to be heading Geffen's way, only to ink a deal with A&M that had been secretly agreed - to the surprise of Geffen and Epic - some months before.

Having recorded the acclaimed 'Screaming Life' and 'Fopp' mini-albums for Sub Pop, Soundgarden were then signed to SST, via the intervention of fellow Washington State band Screaming Trees. "When we started," recalled a distinctly underawed Chris Cornell, "the biggest thing we could have hoped for was to sign with SST. When we finally did, it was just a one-shot, kind of anti-climactic. We knew that we'd be with A&M very soon."

Not that the SST deal was negligible: Soundgarden's album for the label - titled

'Ultramega OK' after the band vetoed Kim Thayil's original suggestion of 'Total Fucking Buttwipe' - ended up with a Grammy nomination. "It was the first time a band out of the scene was getting that much attention," Chris Cornell explained. "Then other bands took some of the focus, which was good as far as we were concerned. When we put out 'Ultramega OK', that was around the time Mudhoneymania happened and the very first demos of Nirvana were heard."

When Axl Rose chose 'Ultramega OK' as one of his albums of the year, the band's overground success was assured. A&M had already advanced Soundgarden some money, well before the SST album came out, "so we're kind of obligated", as Cornell admitted. While the national press tipped the band as a surrogate Led Zeppelin, and Chris Cornell as Jim Morrison reborn, Soundgarden began work on their first album for a major. In the light of the Zepp comparisons, the band toyed with calling it 'John Paul Jones & Ringo', but eventually settled on 'Louder Than Love' - a satire on the dramatic conceits of the metal scene, apparently.

While the band's music was heard in Hollywood films like Cameron Crowe's 'Say Anything' and Hugh Hudson's 'Lost Angels', Soundgarden struggled to keep their punk credentials alive. "They can't throw us into a metal market," said Matt Cameron with fingers knotted, "and A&M isn't a big metal label."

"I rejected all that stuff back at school," Kim Thayil added. "It was this big stupid, sexist, racist thing that didn't rock." But Chris Cornell admitted: "Being aimed at the metal market makes perfect sense, because we've always appealed to that audience, but we've never been exposed to it. It was always more of the college radio market. The Melvins and Malfunkshun and to an extent Green River were sort of the weird bastards of suburban metal."

As the sales of 'Louder Than Love' began to rival those for local metal acts like Queensryche and Metal Church, Soundgarden tried to adjust to their sweeping shift in perspective. "How long can Seattle stay a quaint little music scene?", Chris Cornell anguished. "How long will it stay creative and really different?"

These were questions being asked right across town, as the alternative rock scene in Seattle struggled to relate to the dilemmas of outside infiltration - especially when it came from Seattle's arch enemy, California. Over at Sub Pop, Pavitt and Poneman weren't looking to sign their entire roster over to the major labels: all they wanted was distribution. Unlike Britain, where the country's relatively small size and tightly integrated record industry makes distribution comparatively painless, the indie scene in the States was entirely localised. Kids in Chicago or Memphis could read about the

EVEN ALICE IN CHAIN'S DRUG PROBLEMS CAME FROM A GOLDEN NEEDLE: THEY PROVIDED THE INSPIRATION FOR THE MILLION SELLING 'DIRT' LP.

Sub Pop bands in their imported copies of *Melody Maker*, but they could only buy the records on mail order. In some cities, it was actually easier to find imported pressings of Sub Pop releases from Europe - where they were handled by labels like Tupelo and Glitterhouse - than to find the authentic American article.

"The whole naïve notion that you could have an independent label and have major distribution was very appealing to us. We figured we might be able to take these punk records - these lo-fi, locally produced records - and get them big distribution."

"We're not trying to be a farm team for the majors," Poneman added. "Our gut feeling about major labels is basically that they bumble everything they touch." But while the devil was wining and dining the dynamic duo, they were prepared to listen. By early 1990, it was Sony - the Japanese company who'd taken over the pride of the American record business, Columbia/Epic/CBS - who were showing the keenest interest. The finer points of the deal began to be hammered out - Sony would only take those Sub Pop records they thought they could sell, but would still give the label a large enough advance for them to be able to sign more bands. Not that Poneman and Pavitt were in any doubt that their hottest talents would eventually desert them. In fact, they almost seemed to welcome the idea: "I don't want to have to invest all my capital in keeping one 800-pound gorilla fed," Jonathan quipped in the summer of 1990.

Ultimately, the Sony deal fell through; the major label backed out when it was time to put signatures at the foot of big bundles of paper. "Basically what happened," sighed Poneman when the year-long saga was done, "was we ended up paying out tens of thousands of dollars in legal fees, just pursuing something which, ultimately, I can't believe in my heart of hearts they were ever remotely serious about. And it forced our hand elsewhere. When we said to people, 'Hey guys, we're working on this major label deal', suddenly a lot of bands that we had flimsy contracts and/or no contracts with said, 'Major label distribution, huh? Well, instead of giving us $5,000 for that next record, we want $25,000.' "

Meanwhile, Sony made a move of their own: that summer, they signed up the previously unfancied Seattle band Alice In Chains, while their A&R man, Nick Terzo, announced straightfacedly: "I think the market here is tapped for now. It needs to re-generate itself and re-identify itself musically."

Sony, or at least the Columbia Records division, now had its own alternative rock department, the Progressive Music Marketing Managers. And it was that body that listened to Alice In Chains' "shitty" demo tape, recorded late in 1989. Six months later, the band had signed a seven-album deal; after another six

months, their debut album, 'Facelift', was in the charts, and the 'Man In The Box' single was receiving heavy rotation on MTV, and had been nominated for a Grammy. Even the band's highly publicised drug problems came from a golden needle: they provided the inspiration for their even more successful follow-up LP, 'Dirt'.

Inside and outside the city, there was a feeling that the major Seattle statements had already been made. The hottest bands - Alice In Chains, Mother Love Bone, Soundgarden - had already been signed to the majors, and would presumably move to California at the earliest opportunity. Jack Endino noticed the change: "We had all been very happy. Everyone was doing their thing. We were all surviving. But the original sense of the Seattle scene, as an innocent thing, with people just making a sound that they wanted to make, ended around 1989. A bunch of bands jumped ship, and they got so big it changed things." Poneman and Pavitt were still claiming the credit, but Kim Thayil of Soundgarden wasn't prepared to let that through without a border-pass: "Bruce and Jonathan are the Don Kings of Seattle rock'n'roll. The scene was already there; they just packaged it."

Around March 1990, Nirvana finally began recording their second album at Smart Studios, with Butch Vig as producer. "I think of my new songs as pop songs," Kurt Cobain noted, "as they're arranged with the standard pop format: verse, chorus, verse, chorus, solo, bad solo. There won't be any songs as heavy as 'Paper Cuts' or 'Sifting' on the new record. That's just too boring. I'd rather have a good hook." After several weeks of intermittent sessions, the band had completed six pop songs, and had demo versions of a couple more. Ostensibly, they were intended for Sub Pop: in fact, they were used as demos for a possible major-label deal.

Sub Pop's flirtation with the big leagues had inspired Nirvana to look beyond Seattle - not simply for more money, but because they were afraid that their label might sign a contract with a major that would restrict their own artistic growth. "Another thing is," Kurt complained, "we've never known how many records we've sold at Sub Pop. We don't know how many copies of 'Bleach' we sold. And we weren't being promoted very well. I challenge anybody to find a 'Bleach' ad."

Control was a vital factor to Cobain: frequently on the verge of losing it himself, he recognised its significance to his career. While Mudhoney and Tad toyed with the imagery of backwoods excess and random, instinctive violence, neither band ever came close to relinquishing their hold on what was real and what not. With Nirvana, the lines were much fainter. Despite the fact that Cobain was writing the best songs of his career, it only took a combination of malign circumstances to push him to his limits. At the

New York Pyramid in May, the volcano boiled over, as the club's sound equipment malfunctioned and the wisecracking audience began to call Cobain out. That night, the end-of-show stage-trash was frenzied and desperate: in the audience, Iggy Pop must have recognised a kindred spirit.

A day later, on another night of a seven-week tour in a van without roadies, but with an emergency supply of acid stashed under the dashboard, Cobain borrowed a dress from a member of the audience, and cavorted around the stage with all the glee of a small child.

When the tour was over, Nirvana returned to Seattle to discover that Sub Pop's deal with Columbia had fallen through. It was a period of flux: within a few days, the band's drummer of two years, Chad Channing, had quit. "Chad was more of a jazz drummer," Kurt explained, "and he'd switch to a heavier thing with us. But still he couldn't do it natural." That may be so, but there was an element of bluster to Cobain's remarks, as the departure couldn't have come at a more inconvenient time. The band had dates booked through to the end of the year, an album to complete, and a major label deal to negotiate. For the next few months, rumours about a replacement for Channing filled the British music press, though they went almost unreported in Seattle.

Chad's farewell coincided with the noisy collapse of another American guitar band, Dinosaur Jr, who had been college radio favourites for two or three years. Crossing paths on the alternative club circuit in American and Europe, Cobain and Novoselic had become friends with Dinosaur frontman J Mascis, who had already written the ultimate anthem for uninterested American youth, 'Freak Scene'. The suggestion that he might return to his original instrument, drums, and become one-third of Nirvana, loaded the U.K. press into a frenzy of speculation. An alternative theory had Dan Peters quitting Mudhoney now that Steve Turner was bent on returning to college. Then there was the old standby, Dale Crover of The Melvins, always willing to lend a hand.

It was Dan Peters who landed the job, although his touring commitments with Mudhoney precluded him playing many of Nirvana's North-West shows in the summer. But he was available to record a new single, as Kurt recalled: "Dan was about to leave on tour with Mudhoney, and Tad had just finished in the studio at Reciprocal, so the half-hour after they finished, we went in there and used their equipment and recorded the song." Written only that week, 'Sliver' (originally titled 'Rag Burn') was the song about a child's fear of being left alone with "Grandpa Joe". A majestic record, it appeared on Sub Pop, as usual, backed by the frenetic 'Dive' - which, sexual connotations or not, came from Cobain's lips as a cry of psychic despair.

Listening back to the album tracks they'd

recorded earlier in the year, Cobain and Novoselic made the decision in August to dump them and start again. Briefly, they considered keeping the production duties in-house: "Craig Montgomery, our soundman, wanted a shot at doing the record and we thought we'd give him a chance," Cobain explained. "But it worked out kind of screwy. It was free, though, we didn't pay for it." And the two songs he cut with them, 'Even In His Youth' and 'Aneurysm', eventually found a home on the 12" version of 'Smells Like Teen Spirit'.

The debate over the identity of the band's drummer for their U.K. tour in October 1990 fuelled the news pages of the rock papers for weeks: maybe that was the intention. Eventually, Dan Peters returned to Mudhoney, Novoselic and Cobain fingering his lack of volume as the reason they hadn't retained his services. There was also the small fact that Mudhoney weren't, after all, splitting up: Steve Turner had delayed his return to college for a year, to allow them to record a third album for Sub Pop, and so Peters was required urgently at home.

Dale Crover proved to be unavailable, as The Melvins were also out on the road at the time. But as usual, Nirvana's original mentors came through with 100% support, putting Cobain and Novoselic in touch with the ideal substitute.

Dave Grohl had played drums in the stupidly-titled hardcore outfit Dain Bramage before moving to the more professional Scream, based on the other side of the country in Washington DC. "On the tour we did in the summer of 1990," Grohl recalls, "we found ourselves in Hollywood. The tour sucked: we weren't making very much money, and the bass player started getting back together with his girlfriend over the phone. We woke up one morning and he was gone - she'd wired him money and he flew home. So we were stuck in Hollywood and couldn't find a bass player. While we were there, I talked to Buzz Osborne from the Melvins, and he told me, 'I think Nirvana might call you because they need a drummer.' They didn't call, so instead I called them."

Cobain called Grohl up to Seattle, where they booked a rehearsal studio for the night. Grohl again: "After the first practice, we knew that things were going to work out, because we had the same ideas. They wanted a drummer that played really big drums and hit extremely hard, so things worked out from there. And now Kurt has someone that can sing back-up vocals to the songs."

Grohl moved into Cobain's Seattle apartment: "When I joined the band, I lived with Kurt for eight months. When I first got there, he had just broken up with a girl and was totally heartbroken. We would sit in his tiny, shoebox apartment for eight hours at a time without saying a word. For weeks and weeks this happened. Finally, one night, we were driving

back in the van, and Kurt said to me, 'You know, I'm not always like this'. "

During August and September 1990, Nirvana's relationship with Sub Pop began to collapse. Cobain was no longer being discreet about their intentions: "It's not hard to keep your dignity and sign to a major label. Sonic Youth have been really smart about what they're doing. I feel we're experienced enough to deal with it now. We're changing a little bit, we've been into more accessible pop styles of music for the last two years, and finally we're being able to relieve ourselves of some of that. So we figured we may as well get on the radio and try to make a little bit of money at it."

The Sonic Youth connection was vital. The ultimate alternative band, spouting underground rhetoric and forever sabotaging any commercial intentions with a swift dart into left-field, the New Yorkers had still managed to persuade Geffen Records to take them on board. Their last record before signing the deal was the remarkable 'Daydream Nation', which honed all the punk-rock moves from their earlier albums without diminishing their sprawling canvas, and created an electrifying, compelling set of late Eighties alternative rock music. Geffen must have wanted more of the same, but instead they got the far more playful and quirky 'Goo' - complete with tribute songs to Karen Carpenter and cover art that looked as if it had been drawn by a 10-year-old Andy Warhol.

But though 'Goo' wasn't what they'd been expecting, Geffen still found they could sell it. The mere fact that Sonic Youth albums were in the record chain stores was enough to break the band into the US Top 100 - far beyond the reach of their best indie albums. And Geffen's marketing tactics also brought the band's first single for the label, 'Kool Thing', into heavy rotation on the prime college and alternative radio stations. The revolution wasn't being televised, but it was coming over the airwaves.

Mark Kates was the Director of Alternative Music at the newly-formed Geffen Records subsidiary, DGC. "We signed Sonic Youth about two years before 'Nevermind' came out," he explains, "and Kim Gordon, the bass player and chief business person, said that the next band that DGC - or Geffen at that time, as DGC didn't exist - should sign was Nirvana. So I went out and got their first record and played it a few times I liked it OK, but it didn't really bowl me over. I've never really been a hard rock music fan - not that I'd categorise that album, but just that it sort of goes in that direction. Then I saw them, and the songs started to make some sense. And then I started to see them more, because they were touring with Sonic Youth. When they opened for Sonic Youth at the Palladium, they really blew me away. They showed signs of being a major band who could pull it off and reach a large number of people. When I heard the demos for this album, which

had been around for maybe six months before we started negotiating, I thought they had the potential of being hit songs, while still coming from an edgy atmosphere and appealing to alternative music fans."

For years, Nirvana had been relying on legal advice from local managers like Susan Silver, who'd overseen Soundgarden's leap from Sub Pop and SST to the major labels. Now that DGC were starting to bandy telephone-number figures around, it was time to take care of business. Sonic Youth recommended their manager, Danny Goldberg of Gold Mountain Entertainment, and Nirvana went along. A former publicist who at one time ran Led Zeppelin's Swansong label in the US working closely with Zep's larger than life manager Peter Grant, Goldberg was rooted in the indie scene but he had the experience and clout to handle the steamroller negotiating tactics of the major labels. Goldberg proved to be the ideal handmaiden for Nirvana's dive into the corporate world.

Meanwhile, Sub Pop were floundering. Jon Poneman could see his brightest baby slipping out of reach, but he was relying on honour among gentlemen: "Ethically speaking, I have a signed agreement and I don't want to get fucked over. Having said that, I don't think that Nirvana want to fuck me over. But sooner or later they will have to sit down with us and make a deal. I'm getting bummed out about the lack of communication."

By Christmas, the band were officially reported to be "at loggerheads" with Sub Pop. A week later, the news broke that they'd signed with DGC. Everyone ended up a winner, or so it seemed: Nirvana wolfed a two-album deal with a $250,000 advance (soon rumoured on the indie circuit to be three or four times that figure); Sub Pop took $70,000 as compensation for breaking their contract with the band; and Pavitt and Poneman also won a 3% royalty on Nirvana's records, plus the right to have the Sub Pop logo on every release. The final negotiating point was a minor one: Sub Pop insisted that Nirvana let them have one more single, for which they need only provide one song.

Kurt Cobain explains the circumstances: "We ended up sharing a single with The Fluid. I didn't really want that record to come out, though. I called up Jon at Sub Pop and asked him not to do it. It was just a throwaway, a cover of 'Molly's Lips' by one of our favourite U.K. bands, The Vaselines. I like the song, but the performance just wasn't up to par. But part of our buy-out deal was that single."

"DGC just seemed hip," Chris Novoselic explained when he was asked to justify their move to a major. "If you go to a label like Capitol, they're pretty much dinosaurs. They have no idea where we're coming from at all."

"They have an alternative, young staff," Cobain added. "They have some credentials in the underground."

Though Cobain also insisted that "Maintaining the punk rock ethos is more important to me than anything", the consensus on the punk scene was that Nirvana had sacrificed purity for profit. The hardcore fraternity had never trusted Sonic Youth to begin with - too damn arty, too satirical, not passionate enough about the ideology of punk - and they viewed Nirvana as babes in arms, wooed away from their underground mother with the promise of sticky candy. Distribution, getting the product out to the people, wasn't an issue to the punk community, who were suspicious of any attempt to garner a mass audience. Far better to play for those who had always kept the faith, and let the heretics find their own nirvana.

Kurt Cobain had no illusions of purity: "We're one of those bands that break you in, that eases the middle class into wearing leather eventually," he admitted, almost waiting for the day when their pussy-footing interpretation of punk rock would be swept away by the real thing. He and Nirvana had creative control at DGC, 100% guaranteed: the rest could look after themselves.

1990 ended with the Seattle rock press looking back at a remarkable year for the region, highlighted by the nine Grammy nominations won by local bands (everyone from Kenny G to Soundgarden) and the remarkable MTV breakthrough made by Alice In Chains, then only weeks away from a Grammy nomination themselves. Otherwise, their alternative rock coverage was reserved for Mother Love Bone.

"I've been in training for this all my life," Andy Wood had gushed when Polygram offered his band a deal. By March 1989, their critically lauded 'Shine' EP was in the shops; six months later, after a lengthy cross-country club tour, including a celebratory gig in Seattle with Alice In Chains, they were recording their debut album, Apple. And Andrew Wood was using heroin again. The sessions were completed in October: after a month of hapless denial and self-abuse, Wood checked himself into the Drug/Alcohol Recovery Center in Valley General Hospital. He re-emerged after a month, and began attending regular meetings of Alcoholics Anonymous and Narcotics Anonymous; and he kept writing songs, teasing his bandmates with hints of new tunes that were never committed to tape.

On Friday March 16, 1990, Wood was due in a local bar to meet a new recruit to the Mother Love Bone circle of insiders - a roadie who would double as Wood's personal bodyguard/minder on the road. He never showed. Instead, he injected his first shot of heroin in 106 days, and overdosed. At 10.30pm, he was discovered face down of the bed in his Queen Anne apartment by his longtime girlfriend, Xanna LaFuente - unconscious, a jagged needle puncture in his arm, his face

SOUNDGARDEN MADE THE SHIFT FROM SEATTLE ROCK CLUBS TO THE STADIUM CIRCUIT WITHOUT LOSING A MOMENT'S SLEEP.

deep blue apart from the crimson splash of blood around his mouth. Rushed to Harbor View Medical Center, he was kept on life support systems over the weekend, before doctors reviewed his condition on the Monday, and pronounced him clinically dead. The machines were shut down, and Andrew Wood died a few minutes later.

Wood had described his "toxic shame" to friends: after his death, his family found a poem he'd written two years earlier called *Death*: "I traded life for instant satisfaction/I tipped the scale at 22". As it turned out, he was only two years off the mark. His bandmates were quick to dampen any atmosphere of rock'n'roll glamour attached to his demise: "Andy always knew he was an addict and it was never anything that he thought was cool," commented Stone Gossard. "He really felt ashamed of it."

Polygram held back the release of Mother Love Bone's album for a few weeks, and then put it out anyway. Stone Gossard half-heartedly promoted the record - "It's a memento of how great Andy was at his peak. Maybe through his lyrics, one can get a little insight into why he did what he did." But this particular dream was over: "Mother Love Bone is not going to be around anymore. There's no reason to continue with the name. The only thing for sure is that me and Jeff Ament are going to continue playing together." And so it proved.

Wood's death not only ended one chapter of the Seattle rock story, but instigated another, with effects as yet unseen. Drug-use is so common in rock that no-one mentions it until someone dies. A *Rolling Stone* reporter quoted a prominent Seattle insider after Wood's death: "In the Northwest, heroin is real prevalent. There's something very dark about that city." Bruce Pavitt, however, owned up to another chemical influence on the local rock scene: "Ecstasy is the real sex & drugs & rock'n'roll angle that everyone conveniently overlooks. I was seeing shows all the time on that drug. When Mark Arm was singing for 'Green River', half the time he was blown away on Ecstasy - jumping off columns of speakers and doing really insane shit. There was a lot of 'X' circulating, and that kinda added to the physical power of that slower, heavier groove."

Mark Arm concurred, to a point: "That drug definitely had its place in what was going on, at least for a while. But while we all had our experience with that stuff, I don't think I was nearly as influenced by it as Bruce was."

Heroin, Ecstasy, the acid in Nirvana's touring van, the pot that Matt Cameron was happy to admit was an essential part of the Soundgarden style - even the city's "fucking amazing" magic mushrooms - these all helped to stir media awareness of a physical reality behind the comic-book tales of Seattle

rock'n'roll life. And as soon as one Seattle personality grew large enough, he began to take the rap for all these stories, and more besides.

On the night that the Rock And Roll Hall Of Fame held their annual jamboree in Philadelphia, the Americans began to bomb Baghdad, inaugurating the self-congratulatory tragic farce of the Gulf War. That week, Nirvana began work on their debut for DGC. "When we went to make this record," Chris Novoselic recalled, "I had such a feeling of us versus them. All those people waving the flag and being brainwashed, I really hated them. And all of a sudden they're buying our record, and I just think, 'You don't get it at all'."

The joys of a mass audience were still nine months away when the sessions began, but Kurt Cobain was already preparing himself for compromise: "Butch Vig will be the main producer. But there will be a few songs that we'll pick out to be more commercial, and we'll use other producers for those. We were talking with Scott Litt and Don Dixon - a few different people."

This was not, after all, the voice of the underground, but rather the man who had already compared his band to John The Baptist, smoothing the way for whatever really alternative rock might follow in their wake. The approaches to Litt and Dixon made Nirvana's strategy clear: both men had produced R.E.M., and though their techniques differed, both were skilled at making rock records quirky enough to satisfy critics and college-radio, but smooth enough for Top 40 as well.

In the event, Vig handled the entire sessions for 'Nevermind', at Sound City Studios in Van Nuys, California. The simple choice of location, far away from Seattle, was significant in itself: it allowed Geffen Records to keep a tight watch on the recording process, and to monitor the rising studio costs. 'Bleach' had taken $606 to record; the five weeks of work on 'Nevermind' pushed the budget to around $100,000, around 30% of which (plus expenses) was Butch Vig's cut. (He subsequently renegotiated his fee when the album went platinum.)

"The band comes from a punk-grunge background," Vig explained helpfully, "but Kurt has a strong pop sensibility. He writes great melodies. And there's passion, rage, bewilderment in his voice." And that contrast between melody and rage was exactly what Vig captured on tape. "What I was trying to get was a spontaneous feel," he explained, and the fact that trying to be spontaneous automatically negates spontaneity seems to have eluded him. 'Nevermind' was planned from the start as a commercial record, after all. They could worry about social significance later.

Cobain brought the 1990 demos from the scrapped Sub Pop sessions to Vig, and their arrangements were retained almost intact. The

rest of the album evolved at Sound City, as Dave Grohl explained: "It starts with Kurt, who might have a riff, and he'll bring it into the studio and start playing it. Chris and I will just start following along. We'll jam on it until verses and choruses pop up out of it. It's usually just jamming, there is no actual composing or writing."

Cobain was more dismissive about the act of creation: "We downed a lot of hypodermic cough syrup and Jack Daniels and just lounged on the couch in the recreation area of the studio for days on end, just writing down a few lyrics here and there." That explains where the $100,000 went.

From that process evolved the two most popular songs on the album: 'Smells Like Teen Spirit' and 'Come As You Are'. 'Teen Spirit' (named after a deodorant marketed at a youth audience) was Vig's immediate choice of a single ("It was just blowing me away. I was jumping around the room.") Despite its anthemic title, though, Cobain's lyrics were typically random: like many of his songs, they read like Warholesque transcripts of overheard dialogue, without any plot or location. It took the chorus to simultaneously describe and undercut the status of belonging to a mass audience: "Here we are now/Entertain us/I feel stupid/And contagious". You can almost see the stagedivers.

'Come As You Are' was even more oblique: Cobain let his voice invest the throwaway phrases with meaning, and let the scavengers pick what they would from the fragments of lyrics audible between the guitars. What the song suggested, more than anything else, was incomprehension and anxiety: the chorus was both cathartic and tense, as if to gather up the isolated individuals who heard it and group them into an untidy mass.

"At the time I was writing those songs, I really didn't know what I was trying to say," Cobain admitted towards the end of 1992. "There's no point in my even trying to analyse or explain it." And Jonathan Poneman took his refusal to analyse a step further: "Nirvana are incredibly misinterpreted. Nobody is listening to what this band has to say. The songs' subject matter and lyrics are meaningless. What's meaningful is that they're connecting with people, and saying, you make the decision what are we going to do now?"

Two songs were too important for Cobain to hide their message, however. The first was 'Polly', their scary rapist's-eye-view dialogue of confusion and panic; the second was 'Something In The Way', with its direct references to Cobain's experiences in Aberdeen, sleeping out under the bridge to Cosmopolis, trying to understand why his home didn't feel like home anymore. "I disconnected all the fans and the telephones in the studio," Butch Vig explained. "It was so intimate when

he cut that song. No-one could even breathe." And Cobain's bare acoustic performance closed the album - in theory, at least, for all but the first few thousand 'Nevermind' CDs returned after ten minutes of silence with the cacophonous 'Endless Nameless', a "prank" which didn't fit the running order anywhere else.

When the sessions were over, Nirvana were back out on the road - supporting Screaming Trees in Vancouver, and then preparing for a series of European festival dates supporting Sonic Youth. Elsewhere in Seattle, the divide between the overground success of Alice In Chains, Soundgarden and the remnants of Mother Love Bone, and the increasingly desperate indie scene, was widening.

Even with a sizeable pay-off, Nirvana's departure seriously weakened Sub Pop's financial situation. They'd lost their most marketable commodity, and with the band had disappeared hopes of major-label distribution. The label was still issuing great records - notably singles by L7, Babes In Toyland and Dickless - but Sub Pop was increasingly being regarded as a career-friendly one-stop, a badge of underground authenticity to be waved in the face of the majors.

There were clear signs of desperation. Pavitt and Poneman had been living off the subscriptions for the Sub Pop Singles Club: now they started offering these exclusive 45s to stores, neatly managing to piss off subscribers (who valued their cult status) and retailers, who found themselves inundated with buyers for one single in the series, only to be left with hundreds of unsold copies of the next.

Then there was the Tad fiasco - the record jackets that had to be redesigned, the dispute with Pepsi-Cola, the disappointing sales of '8-Way Santa'. With the Seattle press still reeling from the six-figure advances offered to Nirvana and the rest, Sub Pop started to send their creditors T-shirts with a pointed message: "What part of 'we have no money' don't you understand?"

"We went through a meteoric ascendancy for a few years and we spent and spent and spent," said Jon Poneman apologetically, as Sub Pop laid off longtime employees, cut its distribution service for other local labels, and fielded rumours about their imminent demise. "I don't see how independent distributors stay in business," he added. "Your cost of goods, the cost of the actual wares you are selling, is not that much. We had incredible phone-bills, packaging bills, shipping costs, payroll, and you make so little money. Every now and then, the guy doing the book-keeping would sound the alarms, but Bruce and I had a sense of us growing outward and upward, so we ignored him."

As stories filtered through about old friends arriving at work to find their offices locked, however, Seattle insiders began to chip away at

the Pavitt and Poneman myth. Daniel House, who'd been combining sales work for Sub Pop with running his own C/Z label until Bruce and Jon dispensed with his services, set the blame firmly on their self-indulgence: "There's no good reason they should be in the state they're in now, except for the fact that they spent their money on everything they could. They didn't need to have their American Express Gold Cards to eat two meals a day. They didn't need to fly all over the world as casually and frequently as they did." And House set himself up as successor to the role as fulcrum for the Seattle indie scene: "I want to create a North-West cartel, with selected labels, and run a really tight ship - the way it was at Sub Pop when I was there, but to have even fewer staff."

What saved Sub Pop, in the end, was what created the original myth: their relationship with Mudhoney. Recorded for just $2,000 on eight-track, the band's third LP, 'Every Good Boy Deserves Fudge', sold well enough to pull the label through their debts into some kind of relief. Mixing a new grasp of pop into their garage stew, the album didn't quite reach the mainstream, but it was still Sub Pop's fastest-moving album to date.

Within three months of its release, though, Mudhoney were unable to deny the unthinkable: a shift to a major label. Poneman admitted: "The last I heard, the band wanted to sign to Geffen, purely because Nirvana did." But it was Reprise who eventually captured Mudhoney at the start of 1992. When Tad followed them into a major deal a year later, it marked the departure of all the Seattle bands that Sub Pop had made famous - and vice versa.

On tour across the European festival circuit in the summer of 1991, Nirvana awaited the release of 'Nevermind'. Geffen queried the cover artwork, showing an underwater baby swimming after a dollar-bill on a hook - not for political reasons, but simply because the boy's penis was clearly visible.

The next battle was over the choice of single: Geffen wanted the smooth-edged 'Lounge Act', while producer and band held out for 'Teen Spirit'. On both accounts, Geffen had the choice of cancelling their contract or giving in; so they gave in as discreetly as possible.

The Sonic Youth tour was documented - if that's not too artistic a word - by Dave Markey, whose hand-held video camera produced a deliberately anti-professional 95-minute film, belatedly released early in 1993 under the dubious title, *1991: The Year Punk Broke*. It captures the ambience and self-indulgence of the tour pretty well: just don't look too closely into Kurt Cobain's eyes.

Among the episodes captured on video were Kurt demolishing the amplifier stacks with his head; and a brief encounter between Nirvana's guitarist and the leader of another provocative band, Hole. The woman in question was one Courtney Love: the pair had been spotted together at a Butthole Surfers gig in June, but it took a dose of romantic European air to consummate their relationship into something approaching love.

It transpired that the couple had met before, in the mid-Eighties, when Love was based in Portland, Oregon - the first big city down the coast from Seattle. "Back then, we didn't have any emotion towards each other," Love recalled. "It was like, 'Are you coming over to my house?' 'Are you going to get it up?' 'Fuck you.' That sort of thing." Meeting her again, Cobain had to listen to some "nasty rumours, that she was this perfect replica of Nancy Spungen. That got my attention."

If nothing else, Courtney Love could always be relied upon for a tale, some of which were taller than others. Apparently the daughter (adopted or otherwise) of Grateful Dead roadie Hank Harrison, who chronicled his years with the band in a book, Courtney stressed the mythic rock'n'roll qualifications of her childhood. And the stories keep expanding: Courtney was at Woodstock in 1969, aged 3; she's visible on the back of the Dead's 'Aoxomoxoa'; her parents encouraged her to drop acid before she started school. No rock'n'roll wild child could have imagined a better start.

"I was moved around a lot," Love says of the years that followed. "I have a really dysfunctional family. My mother is really detached. My real father is insane. The only good person in my family is my stepfather. He wasn't in my life that much, though, and I was in institutions. I was in juvenile hall for four years, boarding school for three. I felt really lonely. I was weird. But then I discovered Patti Smith. She saved my life."

Elsewhere, Love recalled: "I was raised by white trash that considered themselves hippies." She spent some of her childhood in Portland, Oregon, where she claims she was given drugs to quiet her unruly nature: "I had Ridilin as a child, which is this drug for hyperactive kids. Some of us turned out really quiet, some have turned out really manic. I'm lucky, I'm one of the manic ones."

In the mid-1970s, she moved with her mother to Australia, and then New Zealand. After that, the stories keep tripping over each other. She was living in a trailer (just like Kurt, strangely enough), while her mother ran through two inter-racial marriages. She was arrested for stealing a Kiss T-shirt from a Woolworths store, and sent to a detention centre ("I learned a lot. To be quite honest, I got into it. It did not have an adverse effect on me."). She started stripping in her mid-teens. She "played sports and beat up people." She shared an apartment with Lydia Lunch. She flew to Japan and danced in bars. She went to the same school as Tom Cruise

and Charlie Sheen. She lived with her therapist. She lived off state benefits. She ran away from her mother. She wouldn't talk to her father. She created a multi-faceted Courtney Love legend.

Finally, some positive sightings: in 1982, she was in Liverpool, where she'd paid her way from her earnings in Japan. At the age of 16, she was hanging out with the luminaries of the Northern rock scene - seen constantly with Julian Cope, fighting Pete Burns in a bar, inspiring the Teardrop Explodes single 'When I Dream'. "Just because I was with Julian," she recalled three years later, "everyone has since assumed we were lovers." Cope waited ten years before delivering his own verdict: in October 1992, he took out music press ads to assault a variety of targets, including Ms Love: "Free us from Nancy Spungen fixated heroin a-holes who cling to our greatest rock groups and suck out their brains," he wrote, suggesting he was a trifle jealous that one of his protégées was now more famous than he was.

From Liverpool, Love returned to Portland. Over the next few years, she made a living as a stripper whenever she needed dollar bills: "It was a totally normal thing to do: every girl in a band did it so they could buy guitars and amps." And she made friends with other girls who wanted to be rock'n'roll stars, like Kat Bjelland and Jennifer Finch. Those three formed Sugar Baby Doll around 1984 ("We wore pinafores and played 12-string Rickenbackers - it was a disaster").

"Jennifer and I were not into it," remembered Kat of this attempt to upstage The Bangles. "We wanted to play punk rock. Courtney thought we were crazy. She hated punk then." Whatever the details, Finch introduced Love to cult film director Alex Cox, who was preparing to film the rock soap drama, Sid And Nancy. "He met me and put his arm around me, and said the most subversive thing he could think of. He was foisting me on the world. That was when I was really overweight, too," glowed Courtney gratefully.

To Julian Cope's undoubted disgust, Love didn't get the role of Nancy Spungen in Cox's movie, anymore than Kurt Cobain was offered the chance to be Sid. Instead, she played a punk cameo, before winning a more substantial role - and her first hint of fame - in Cox's next project, the alcohol-fuelled mock-Western, Straight To Hell.

"The film's about sexual tension," Cox explained on location. "Here are 750 guys in this town, and only five women. No-one ever gets laid. It's about the cult of machismo. Also, the sexual roles are all fucked up. Why shouldn't the guys get all tearful and weepy, while the women stand around spitting and chewing tobacco? Women aren't an archetype. They're tougher than men."

Cleverly condensing the entire grunge anti-sexist ethic into one paragraph, Cox cast

Courtney Love as Velma, whom she described as "a white trash pregnant bitch, some weird hillbilly from an incestuous background who's fascinated with charms and magic. She's into tackiness." At the age of 20, she was already typecast.

The film was shot on the southern edge of the Sierra Nevada in Spain. While the film's real stars - rockers on vacation like Elvis Costello, The Pogues and Joe Strummer - evaded the attentions of visiting reporters, Courtney Love was only too eager to be exposed. She told one writer that she felt like "a living ley-line", another that she was working her way through the crew, sleeping with "the director, the director of photography, the assistant director..."

"I was sexless," she admitted in 1992. "People said Alex and I were a couple because that's how they explain his interest in me. During that time, I did not sleep with anybody. I was fat, and when you're fat you can't call the shots. It's not you with the power."

The power of publicity was something she understood, however, and the interviews she gave in Spain show her creating a 'Courtney Love' persona which has survived to this day. Back in the States when the film flopped, she reconsidered rock'n'roll. Between Sid And Nancy and Straight To Hell, she and Kat Bjelland had moved to Minneapolis to find The Replacements, whose 'Unsatisfied' had been the pair's Portland anthem. Now she returned to Minneapolis, joining Kat in the first line-up of Babes In Toyland. The pair soon fell out: "After Kat kicked me out of my own band," she recalled, "I got really depressed. I moved back to Portland and I was just going to be a stripper for the rest of my life and never have a band again. But I heard Mudhoney's 'Touch Me I'm Sick' one night, and I was saved. I knew that I could scream on cue like that."

She briefly settled in New York, auditioning for the Last Exit To Brooklyn movie and playing Jean Harlow in Michael McClure's often-banned play, The Beard. Unable to find a suitable band, she resumed stripping, and heard Sonic Youth's Sister for the first time. A year or so later, she returned to California, where she took out an ad in the Recycler: "I want to start a band. My influences are Big Black, Sonic Youth and Fleetwood Mac."

Among those who replied to the request were drummer Caroline Rue (whose trailer park upbringing triggered Love's interest), bassist Jill Emery, and guitarist and token male Eric Erlandson. Love christened the band Hole - claiming on more than one occasion that she took the name from Euripides' play Medea ("it's about the abyss that's inside"). Not that she was exactly unaware of the sexual connotations, of course.

Somewhere along the way, Love got married to James Moreland, the cross-dressing lead singer of LA punks, The Leaving Trains. The

THE SHORT-LIVED FOUR-MAN NIRVANA LINE-UP WITH DRUMMER CHAD CHANNING AND SECOND GUITARIST JASON EVERMAN WHO WENT ON TO ENDURE AN EQUALLY BRIEF STAY AS GUITARIST WITH SOUNDGARDEN.

HOLE, PRIME EXPONENTS OF WHAT
(MALE) JOURNALISTS WERE QUICK
TO LABEL 'FOXCORE'.

band's songs have a stale air of casual sexism, which can scarcely have delighted Love; the only saving grace was that the marriage took place in Las Vegas, which qualifies for extra points for tackiness. More a whim than a life-changing decision, the marriage was forgotten within days - important only when it had to be dissolved so that Love could marry Kurt Cobain. In July 1990, Hole issued their first single, 'Retard Girl'. From its ambivalent imagery - was that cover shot innocent or a coy reference to child abuse? - to its savage sound, it announced the arrival of an unforgettable rock voice. It also coincided (or not, depending on whether you accept Courtney Love as the catalyst of the entire episode) with a band-generated, media-fuelled 'explosion' of female punk talent.

As they gradually came to realise, Love and her cohorts were treading a path which had first been hacked out during the post-punk era. Building on the inspiration of the punk group, The Slits, British bands like The Raincoats, Girls At Our Best, The Au Pairs and the Delta Five gave women at least an equal voice on a rock scene still dominated by male and female stereotypes. For the first time, women were able to create music which wasn't imprisoned by what other women had done in the past, but equally wasn't a lame attempt to mirror male rock. Small wonder that Kurt Cobain returned to these lone 45s from the late Seventies and early Eighties when the second wave of women rock bands threatened to overturn the comfortable carriage of the mainstream in the early Nineties.

It was Thurston Moore, the over-aged comedian of Sonic Youth, who coined the phrase 'foxcore' to describe the class of 1990. "It's the future," he burbled. "Any babe who rocks out steams up the fucking scene. Dudes rock only because chicks want them to rock. The whole concept of rock'n'roll was created by chicks for dudes to do, to entertain them and satisfy them. Down the road of rock'n'roll history, you started getting dudes dressing up as chicks when you got the glam thing. They were trying to get closer to their origin, which was chick-based. You got guys wearing eyeshadow, lipstick and tight pants. Now, finally, you have this whole new generation of chicks taking over what they created."

It was difficult to know what to object to first - the mock inarticulacy of Moore's conversation, the banality of his argument, the near-sexism of the 'foxcore' term. But the label stuck, and soon the British music press - particularly *Sounds*, who concocted a list of New Wave American Babes - were confining women rockers into a playpen marked 'exotic'.
Alongside Hole, Babes in Toyland, L7, Dickless (all three having issued singles on Sub Pop), STP, PMS (great name) and the Lunachicks were all forced into the new 'scene'. By Christmas 1990, *Melody Maker* were calling it

'vixcore' - which really wasn't any better, boys. And by then, the press spotlight was switching back and forth between Hole, Babes In Toyland and L7.

What the papers didn't realise for another year or more was that all three bands shared a past - in Sugar Baby Doll. While Love had formed Hole, Kat Bjelland had retained control of Babes In Toyland, and Jennifer Finch, their friend from Portland, had started L7. Kat denied talk of a movement: "Suddenly there are all these other girl bands, which is really cool, but it's not like 'Hey, sisterpower', or anything like that. We're just three strong personalities who happen to be women."

She claimed later that "Babes In Toyland fits into the retarded, fun-loving teenager category", but by the time they'd escaped from the amateur dramatics of 'Spanking Machine' in 1990 and cut the bittersweet 'To Mother' album, their feminist credentials were too strong to miss. The band recorded another powerful album, 'Fontanelle', in 1992, but by then the press were just as interested in what Kat had said about Courtney in *Vanity Fair*. By the end of that year, the Babes had split (temporarily, they said) and Kat had moved to Seattle with her husband Stuart, where they were planning to work as a duo called Katstu.

Jennifer Finch's band, L7, deliberately evaded feminist stereotyping. Their image was excess; their PR suggested month-long orgies of sex and drugs, where innocent men would be stripped of their decency and potency and then cast aside in the hunt for fresh blood. Not for nothing did the band start out with a song called 'Bite The Wax Tadpole'. "We formed L7 so we could get laid!" screamed guitarist Suzi Gardner, and male rock fans ran a mile.

At the same time, L7 actively supported women's rights more energetically than the other 'foxcore' bands. Their early recordings included 'Miss 45', in which a woman turned to prostitution to enable her to revenge herself upon her rapist; and 'Diet Pill', about wife battering. Around the end of 1991, they formed Rock For Choice with the Fund For The Feminist Majority organisation, and enlisted the support of Nirvana, Hole, Pearl Jam and even Aerosmith for money-raising concerts. "We happen to be feminists, but that's not the basis of the band," declared guitarist Donita Sparks, but their actions suggested otherwise. Meanwhile, they outgrunged every band in America with their 'Smell The Magic' (complete with wonderfully tasty poster) and 'Bricks Are Heavy' albums - the latter produced by Butch 'Nevermind' Vig.

Beneath the mainstream - both the Babes and L7 were signed to major labels by 1992 - there lurked a healthy women's underground. "A couple of years ago," said Gilly of Calamity Jane, "I felt very discouraged about the whole grunge thing, because it was so male-dominated, all that Sub Pop stuff. The attitude

that was coming out of Seattle was a Seventies male rocker attitude. But all that's changing now."

In Seattle, women-only bands like Bratmobile, Seven Year Bitch and Courtney Love (the band, not the woman) began to play local club gigs, and organise their own anti-industry structure. Musically, they were often directly inspired by Seattle's male rock music - particularly after the success of Nirvana - but their politics were much closer to the surface. Early in 1991, Bratmobile crossed the country from Washington State to Washington DC, where they met another female band, Mecca Normal.

Enlisting the aid of Bikini Kill's Kathleen Hanna, a vague movement was formed, christened 'Riot Girl', with a fanzine to match. Meetings were held locally every week, and slowly the teen feminist momentum spread, until similar fanzines and co-ops were springing up all over America. By the summer of 1992, 'Riot Girl' had become 'Riot Grrrl' and had made (thanks to Sally Margaret Joy) the pages of *Melody Maker* - where guess who, Everett True, was also championing the cause.

One of the seminal (not the best word in the circumstances, I know) events in the development of this women's network was the International Pop Underground, a festival held in Olympia, Washington, in August 1991. Day one was 'Girly Day' - "girly day, for girls, by girls and about girls in rock full on - boys come and see what rock is all about", boasted the publicity) - when L7, Bikini Kill, Bratmobile and many more played. To celebrate the event, Calvin Johnson and Candice Peterson's K Records label in Olympia issued a series of Grrrl-flavoured compilations - including one, 'Kill Rock Stars', to which Nirvana donated an out-take from the 'Bleach' sessions. Kurt Cobain gave the movement regular exposure in interviews; Courtney Love, though distancing herself from the separatists, followed suit; and rock was given its most overt feminist movement ever, the fall-out from which has yet to settle. Interestingly, most of the 'Riot Grrrl' and (dread word) 'foxcore' bands were playing musical forms thought to be exclusively male - punk, metal, hard rock and grunge. Maybe that was the biggest revolution of all.

Shortly before Kurt and Courtney were out on the town with the Butthole Surfers, Hole issued their second single - the astringent sexual threat of 'Dicknail'. Then they began work on their début album, co-produced by Love's spiritual godmother, Kim Gordon of Sonic Youth, and Gumball leader Don Fleming. Before each vocal take, Fleming dosed Love with a fresh shot of whiskey: only then could she strip away protective layers and match the confrontational anguish of her lyrics in her voice.

"A lot of the pain in Hole's music is mine," Love admitted, "and that's because this is the way I choose to express it. I'm very possessive of my pain. I used to express it in ways that were terrible for other people. But a lot of the album is just narrative. The songs still feel like catharsis, still feel like exorcism, still feel really good to sing, but it's still narrative. I'm not a character actress, I'm a songwriter."

Contradicting herself almost every sentence, Courtney Love decided the question of her emotional and sexual involvement in her songs every time she opened her mouth to sing. The brazen degradation of 'Teenage Whore' - assumed as autobiography by most critics, friendly or otherwise - mightn't have been a true-life confession, but it dripped the raw blood of experience. And the rest of the album, as emotionally draining a listening experience as anything rock has ever produced, matched it.

Regardless of the narrative truth of 'Pretty On The Inside', its psychic realism convinced Love's public. She was immediately typecast as the dark heroine of her own songs - sluttish, sick, suffering, a bruised temptress masquerading as a baby doll. And once you start to display that kind of imagery before the world, you better have the strength to keep it up, or the world will chew you up and spit you out as dead meat.

Someone attracted by the smell was Madonna, whose Maverick Entertainment talent organisation began to make tentative advances in Courtney Love's direction. Initially flattered, Love soon replied with cynicism: "This really insane, weird thing happened with her. I think she wanted to buy not only us but all these underground bands she doesn't have a clue about, like Pavement and Cell. I pretty much only had one in-depth conversation with her, and she was going on about being a revolutionary. I'd sold like two records compared to her, and I didn't feel competitive or anything, but I felt like I'd hate her to be the person who put our records out. When you fuck with Jesus or God or whoever she thinks she is, you pay a price."

By early 1992, the new Jesus or God was DGC, whose A&R Head Gary Gersh signed Hole to a deal that gave the band a reported one-million dollar advance - four times what the same label had offered Nirvana. Beating out Def American, Arista and Virgin, DGC were aware that Hole were signed to City Slang, the indie who'd issued 'Pretty On The Inside', for two more albums. The entire deal rested on Love still being a significant figure in 1994 or 1995: maybe the kudos of capturing the woman who the press were naming 'the Queen of Grunge' was worth a million of any fool's money.

The week that 'Pretty On The Inside' reached the shops, Geffen issued Nirvana's 'Nevermind'. Gary Gersh sums up the

company's expectations: "Anyone who tells you they knew how successful this record would be is not telling the truth. The truth of the matter is that I thought when we finished that it was an exquisite record for what it was. We always anticipated over a long period of time the record doing very well, selling maybe 500,000 copies."

To facilitate that success, Geffen shipped out promo copies of 'Smells Like Teen Spirit', having been convinced by Vig and the band that it was the most commercial track on the album. "The song was first played on the commercial alternative stations, like K-ROCK here in Los Angeles," explains DGC's Director of Alternative Music, Mark Kates. "It was only being played at night, but it provoked such an incredible reaction, just even on one play, and that more than anything else is the story behind its success."

Peter Baron, from Geffen's Video Promotions department, takes up the story: "We gave the record to MTV just a week or two after the track went to radio. Little did we realise that there was a lot of understanding of what Nirvana was, and what they were about, internally at MTV. There was this excitement and passion - not really from the head executives, but some of the lower people, who were screaming for the record even before we gave them the video."

"Excitement and passion" aren't things you usually associate with a TV station, even one masquerading as a haven for alternative music like MTV. What the station recognised was the passion that 'Teen Spirit' fired in its audience - as reflected in requests for repeat plays of the video. MTV launched it in their 'Buzz Bin' in September 1991; it was soon being aired five or six times a day. Ironically, Cobain declared the video "a hell of an embarrassment". But beyond its standard indie rhetoric - fast cuts, swirling camerawork, superimposed effects - it captured some sense of inarticulate rage and despair which chimed with those who saw it. As Mark Kates at DGC put it, "To a hell of a lot of disenfranchised people, this record is incredibly important."

'Smells Like Teen Spirit' is a classic 'alternative' rock record. That needs an explanation: 'alternative' is a marketing term designed to satisfy the customers' elitist urges, while warning the accountants that sales might not match the boundless extravagances of the mainstream rock market. Above all, the 'alternative' badge is a form of control. It denotes a record that is too loud or violent for 'adult' rock stations, who might be able to cope with the playful mock-passion of U2 but not the guitar fury of hungry youth. But the mere fact that a record is accepted for 'alternative' airplay or TV broadcast shows that it is not a direct threat to the smooth operation of the network. Genuinely subversive records - which either don't conform to audience expectations, or which challenge accepted taboos, social, sexual

or political - don't make 'alternative' playlists; they don't get played on the radio at all. In that sense, Sonic Youth's' 1991: The Year Punk Broke' is a quintessential 'alternative' document: in its entirely predictable childishness and planned amateurishness, it conforms exactly to what its consumers desire - the illusion of revolution within the safe boundaries of commercial appeal.

And by that criterion, Nirvana is an alternative rock band *par excellence* - the kind of group, as you'll remember Kurt said, "that break you in, that eases the middle class into wearing leather eventually". With 'Teen Spirit', leather had never seemed so enticing, or so liberating.

Nirvana realised something strange was happening when Axl Rose wanted a backstage pass for a show in Los Angeles; the band happily turned him down. But they were back in Europe when 'Nevermind' climbed the U.S. album charts, and pulled the 'Teen Spirit' single - two months or more after MTV first aired the video - in its wake.

Within a few days, the band had lost any semblance of control over their career. There was a brief moment of exhilaration, and then panic. "We wanted to do as good as Sonic Youth," Chris Novoselic explained. "We thought we'd sell a couple hundred thousand records at the most, and that would be fine. Next thing you know, we go Top 10. I wish we could have a time machine and go back to two months ago. I'd tell people to get lost."

The reference was sufficiently vague to include anyone and everyone - MTV, perhaps, or radio, the record company too. And Guns N'Roses fans, for sure: "I'm not proud of the fact that there are a bunch of those kids who are into our music," whined Cobain, rapidly learning that when you offer your wares to the public, you can't choose your audience.

By December 1991, Cobain was suffering throat problems and cancelling shows. He was also offering cryptic comments on the band's chainmail grip on his future: "I'm under contract. I'm in fear of having to go to court if I were to leave the band." Back in the States, he dyed his hair purple as a vain gesture of rebellion. After Christmas, the band trashed their equipment noisily during an MTV show; then a few days later, they repeated the auto-destruct games on *Saturday Night Live*, after which Cobain and Novoselic indulged in an audience-provoking French kiss.

Early in January 1992, 'Nevermind' reached No. 1 on the American album charts, newly adjusted to reflect record sales rather than company hype. Novoselic summed up the group's manifesto: "All we are saying is 'Be aware'. There's a lot of information out there. Use it." And information isn't all that was on offer.

That month, Kurt Cobain and Courtney Love began to use heroin.

Journalist J.D. McCulley interviewed Cobain shortly after Christmas, and noted that his subject was not at his best: "The pinned pupils, sunken cheeks and scabbed, sallow skin suggest something more serious than mere fatigue," he noted. Then on February 24, in Waikiki, Hawaii, Kurt married Courtney, who by this time already knew she was pregnant. What happened in those two months after Christmas sparked a flurry of accusations and justifications that may yet end in the law courts.

"We went on a binge," admitted Courtney when she was quizzed about the couple's activities in the early days of 1992. "We did a lot of drugs. We got pills and then we went down to Alphabet City and we copped some dope. Then we got high and did *Saturday Night Live*. After that, I did heroin for a couple of months."

That was enough to convince *Vanity Fair* journalist Lynn Hirschberg that Love had been using heroin when she already knew she was pregnant. Her story appeared in the September issue of the glossy New York magazine. At first, *Vanity Fair* chose to promote the issue by fingering Love as "a charismatic opportunist and proud of it", with the heroin accusations buried in a later paragraph. But it was Love's apparent admission that she'd endangered her unborn child's life which provoked a worldwide reaction. "It was a bad time to get pregnant," Love was quoted as saying, "and that appealed to me." And 'insiders', those perennial suppliers of juicy tales, were reported to have visited the Cobains at home, revealing "it's a sick scene in that apartment, but lately Courtney's been asking for help". The article also suggested that heroin use had been a regular part of Love's life for some years.

Faced with what they knew would be a public outcry, the Cobains released an official statement the day before the issue reached the news-stands. "The *Vanity Fair* article on Courtney Love contains many inaccuracies and distortions," it began, "and generally gives a false picture of both of us, including our attitude about our bands, other musicians and drugs... The most upsetting allegation is one by an un-named source which suggests that Courtney was doing heroin after she knew she was pregnant. We unequivocally deny this. As was made clear to Ms Hirschberg by Courtney and others close to her, she and Kurt did experiment with drugs early in their relationship which they now deeply regret... As soon as Courtney found out she was pregnant she immediately contacted an obstetrician and a doctor specializing in chemical dependency and has been under their care since then and has been assured she can expect to have a healthy baby... Because we were stupid enough to do drugs at one brief time, we realize that we opened ourselves up to gossip by people in the rock world who want desperately to pretend they have some 'inside' information on famous

people. We never dreamed that such gossip would be reported as if it were true."

A week later, on August 19, 1992, Frances Bean Cobain was born in a Los Angeles hospital. For the press, it was open season. Most sensational of all the media reports of the event was a scurrilous piece of 'journalism' in the American tabloid, the *Globe*. "Rock star's baby is born a junkie", screamed the headline, while a strap-line gloated: "They've got money & fame but no damn heart". Dividing pictures of Cobain and Love was a heartrending shot of a premature baby, perhaps only minutes old, fastened to life support systems. It seemed to support the accusation in the headline, until you read the caption: "Tragic Frances Bean Cobain is going through agonizing withdrawal. She will suffer shivering, cramps and muscle spasms - just like this drug baby."

The *Globe*'s story suggested that Love had continued her drug habit until two weeks before the baby was born. "A source close to the couple" - a wonderful euphemism for "someone eager for a quick buck" - claimed that Courtney arrived at the hospital "so spaced out she had no idea what she was doing... (she) was totally incoherent... she would demand food, eat some and then throw the rest against the wall..."; and so it went on. When the worst of these accusations were repeated in an English tabloid newspaper, Love threatened a libel suit.

Eager to regain the momentum, Cobain gave an interview to Robert Hilburn, one of America's most respected music writers. "I've been accused of being a junkie for years," he admitted. "I've had this terrible stomach problem for years and that has made touring difficult. People would see me sitting in the corner by myself looking sick and gloomy. The reason is that I was trying to fight against the stomach pain, trying to hold my food down. People looked (at) me and assumed I was some kind of addict. I did heroin for three weeks. Then I went through a detox program... to straighten myself out again. That took a really long time - about a month."

The trouble was, Cobain's reliability in medical manners had already been open to question. Back in 1991, he'd chosen to tell interviewers "I'm a narcoleptic", a story repeated in countless stories about the band, only to admit a year or so later that it was a fabrication. "I don't have narcolepsy," he told *Melody Maker*'s Everett True. "It's the only defence mechanism I have."

So Cobain's denials and Love's protestations were treated with a pound or two of salt - until, that is, the couple appeared before photographers with their baby, who conformed to all the stock adjectives - healthy, bouncing, smiling - that the tabloids reserve for the infants of those they admire. Any trace of drug addiction in young Frances Bean Cobain was impossible to detect. Her parents appeared equally ebullient, even if their subsequent interviews necessarily returned time and again to the precise details of their "binge" and the media outrage it had stirred.

The Cobains' three-week "binge" coincided with what the English press were quick to term 'Nirvanamania'. 'Nevermind' rapidly went platinum: within six months, it had sold four million copies in the U.S.A. alone. 'Smells Like Teen Spirit' was followed by a series of singles pulled from the album - 'Come As You Are', 'Lithium', 'In Bloom'. In the midst of the drug dramas, Nirvana toured the world, visiting Australia, New Zealand, Japan and (of course) Hawaii. When the tour was over, the couple went home-shopping, eventually settling on a woodland house outside Seattle.

Cobain wasn't the only Nirvana member bending under the pressure. Novoselic owned up to a drink problem, while drummer Dave Grohl was portrayed as a rampant indulger in the pleasures of the flesh. It was an ideal time for Nirvana to record a song called 'Oh, The Guilt', intended for a split single, in an arrangement that harked back to the less complicated times when they were still an indie band.

"We were just hanging around with the Jesus Lizard," Novoselic explained, "we played a few shows with them, and we said we should do a split single together. And this one actually materialised. We got on the ball and made sure it was seen through to the end. We recorded it in Dave's room-mate's basement. We just hammered these songs out, and said, 'That's a good one for the split single!'" Nearly a year later, DGC finally gave clearance for 'Oh, The Guilt' to be released, albeit only as a worldwide limited edition.

Months before the heroin story broke, Nirvana were still the subject of myth in the early summer of 1992. First there was a laughable comic-book history of the band. "We're being totally raped by these people," Cobain complained. "We have no control over this stuff." A month later, it was the oldest fiction in rock: Kurt was supposedly dead in a car crash. Instead, he was back out on the road, reaching Belfast in June, where he scuffled with a bouncer and collapsed the following day with severe stomach pains. "Everyone's been saying 'overdose'," said an official spokesman, "but there's nothing in it"

"People thought we'd self-destruct," Novoselic told Everett True, "but we haven't. I kind of thought that too, because we took off in such a fury. I was messed-up drunk. Then we had a three-month period where we chilled out and everything was OK. It seems we're a lot tamer now, almost going through the motions."

Observers of their shows that summer agreed. Those 'insiders' resurfaced to suggest that Cobain was close to the edge, though it wasn't clear what of. Everyone was adamant, though, that the band had lost their enthusiasm for the road. Unable to play new songs because they'd be bootlegged within the hour, they trudged through their back catalogue, playing as if by memory, and trashing their gear like wind-up dolls. Cobain was as aware as anyone that "last year's shows were way better": he began talking about augmenting the band, bringing in Buzz Osborne as another guitarist; of "starting another band with Mark Arm and Eric from Hole"; or, more often than not, of quitting Nirvana altogether.

Cobain returned home from tour to discover that his stock of song lyrics and poetry had been destroyed when a broken water-main flooded his Seattle apartment. Two weeks later, the *Vanity Fair* story broke. Then came the baby; then an appearance at the MTV Video Awards, where Nirvana briefly threatened to defy a network ban on a new song called 'Rape Me' before giving in and performing 'Lithium'. While would-be biographers - more of whom later - started sifting through the Cobains' trash in search of incriminating evidence, Courtney and Kurt began to fantasise about the dream of anonymous life in a small town in Oregon.

Cobain wasn't the only Seattle star fracturing under the weight of publicity. In the summer of 1992, Eddie Vedder celebrated the triumphal rise of another new Seattle band, Pearl Jam, by disintegrating in public midway through a tumultuous European tour. Cobain had little time for Pearl Jam - "the curse of corporate rock", he called them - but Vedder's plight wasn't something to crow about.

Vedder pulled himself around soon enough, and within a couple of months Nirvana's 'Nevermind' - the alternative rock sensation of the Nineties, albeit on a major label - had been overhauled by Pearl Jam's 'Ten', which racked up its four-million sales by the late summer of 1992. Pearl Jam didn't claim to be punks, but with the cream of the Sub Pop class of 1988 already signed to majors, punk was getting hard to define.

For all Cobain's jibes, Pearl Jam had punk credentials. The band emerged from the wreckage of Mother Love Bone, who had disbanded the week that their début album, 'Apple', reached the shops - a month after singer Andrew Wood's heroin OD. The remains of the group were dropped from their obligations to Mercury; but Jeff Ament and Stone Gossard, as promised, kept playing together. In the fall of 1990, they began cutting demos for a tribute project to Wood - drawing in not just Gossard's schoolfriend, Mike McCready, but also Chris Connell and Matt Cameron of Soundgarden. As Temple Of The Dog, they recorded an album for A&M late in 1990: in the wake of Pearl Jam's success, it eventually went platinum in 1992.

That was always intended as a sideline. As early as June 1990, though, Ament and Gossard started assembling a new band. McCready and Cameron were ever-present at these demo sessions, which spawned a tape of instrumentals, fuelled as much by the emotional pull of Wood's death as by their shared love of Soundgarden and early 70s hard rock. A copy of the tape found its way to ex-Chili Peppers/Redd Kross drummer Jack Irons, living down the coast in San Diego. In turn, he passed it on to Eddie Vedder, vocalist with a half-hearted rock band called Bad Radio. He was working nights as a night porter at a gas station: returning from a shift, he went surfing like a true Californian, returned home focused by lack of sleep, and wrote three sets of melodies and lyrics to the Ament/Gossard demos. Two weeks later, Vedder was in a Seattle basement, watching the Temple Of The Dog project come together, and contributing to the first full rehearsal sessions of Ament and Gossard's new band.

They started out as Mookie Blaylock, named after the point guard with basketball team, the New Jersey Nets. When lawyers raised the issue of copyright, they became Pearl Jam - after the peyote-based preserve that Vedder's great-grandmother, Pearl, used to serve her husband as a hallucogenic post-prandial surprise. They were managed by Kelly Curtis, who'd supervised Mother Love Bone's career; and she negotiated them a deal with Sony, who'd already signed another Curtis outfit, Alice In Chains.

Their debut album, 'Ten', emerged just before Christmas 1991: for most of the next year, they were on the road, hampered only by Vedder's need to catch breath after the speed of his ascent to arenas and stadiums. Passionate, yet always controlled, Pearl Jam epitomised the new sound of Seattle. With Vedder leading them like a doomed revolutionary from centre-stage, the band embraced a messianic aura. Their music, said Ament, had "a theme of wanting to reach out for life and make the most of each and every day. I hope it's a message of optimism." No wonder Cobain was appalled.

The simultaneous release of 'Nevermind' and 'Ten' alerted the most airless corners of the corporate rock galaxy to the fact that something was happening in Seattle. It wasn't just Nirvana and Pearl Jam: there was Soundgarden, whose 'Badmotorfinger' album in 1991 finally transported their stadium-bound hard rock into its natural arena; Alice In Chains, who followed their million-selling debut with the multi-million 'Dirt'; Screaming Trees, who followed years of semi-popular releases with a major-label breakthrough, again via Sony; even Mother Love Bone and Temple Of The Dog, exhumed from the tombs of the past for an unreal second life as progenitors of Pearl Jam. The sound of Seattle had no musical unity beyond men and

PEARL JAM, VIEWED AS TRAITORS TO THE PUNK
ESTABLISHMENT FOR THEIR UNASHAMED
ESPOUSAL OF MAINSTREAM ROCK.

guitars; but it was translated into a movement by media observers desperate for a filing system that could make sense of the 1990s rock diaspora.

"It's the way that people are perceiving the whole scene right now that gets kind of annoying," said Soundgarden's Matt Cameron. "They don't understand the history of it or the importance of it. There's this blind acceptance for any band from Seattle. The time I get really miffed is when people think of all the Seattle bands out of chronological order. We were one of the first ones to sign a major-label deal to come out of that amazingly fertile scene that peaked around '86, '87. And here we are - we're still doing it. But they think that Nirvana's the first band from Seattle."

Any sense of underground unity that had survived from the days when there were no more than 200 people at any Seattle club gig had dissolved once those figures were multiplied by a hundred or a thousand. It was as if 'Seattle' stood for some kind of Christ-like purity, sacrificed in the name of Money: the former disciples milled at the foot of the cross, each claiming to own the most authentic relic, squabbling among themselves while no-one noticed that the body had disappeared. Only in this version of the Easter story, the disciples didn't face years of persecution: like Judas Iscariot with his conscience surgically removed, they were rewarded for their apostasy with untold wealth, tinged only with the faint itch of guilt at what they'd left behind.

No sooner was 'Seattle' buried - celebrated, perhaps, in Soundgarden's inevitably controversial 'Jesus Christ Pose' - than Hollywood unleashed the movie. The film was former *Rolling Stone* writer Cameron Crowe's *Singles*, premiered in September 1992. A rites-of-passage romance, set somewhat improbably in the Seattle grunge scene, the movie was greeted by purists as a sickening exploitation of the city and its music; and, of course, it cleaned up at the box office.

But as ever, the politics of the situation were more tangled than they appeared. Director Crowe had already used songs by Mother Love Bone and Soundgarden on the soundtrack of his 1989 movie, *Say Anything*. He'd lived in Seattle since marrying local musician Nancy Wilson, of the 'Canadian' rock band Heart. And he'd been hanging out with musicians like Jeff Ament and Stone Gossard since 1988. Himself little older than the musicians in Seattle's leading bands, Crowe envisaged a movie that would capture the self-generating vitality of the city's alternative rock scene. He completed the initial script early in 1990 - around the same time that Nirvana made their first attempts to follow up 'Bleach'. It took another year to secure studio backing, but by February 1991, Crowe was ready to begin rehearsals.

The first day of shooting was on March 11,

1991: exactly a month later, the set was honoured by a visit from alternative rock gods Sonic Youth, escorted by a proud Mark Arm from Mudhoney. Alice In Chains were filmed in concert at a yet-to-be-opened Seattle club, Desoto's; by May, initial shooting was finished. And in November, Crowe held the first preview screening of the movie in Seattle.

It took another ten months for the film to reach the outside world. Previewed by its Seattle all-star soundtrack album, which included solo outings from Chris Connell and ex-Replacement Paul Westerberg, alongside Mudhoney, Alice In Chains and Pearl Jam, *Singles* consolidated the 'It Happened In Seattle' vibe. Though critics sniggered at the cleanliness and adult ambitions of its main characters, as played by the likes of Bridget Fonda and Matt Dillon, the young American public lapped up its romantic complications and vaguely rebellious setting. Scene-spotters could also enjoy the cameo appearances of Pearl Jam and Tad in various on-location episodes of the movie.

The Austin-based 'Generation X' documentary *Slackers*, which opened around the same time as *Singles*, actually came closer to unearthing the real ethos of Seattle, while earlier movies set in the faintly eerie North-West, from *Streetwise* to *My Own Private Idaho*, caught the city's scarily bracing spirit of isolation. But *Singles* will likely go down in history as the authentic Seattle movie, swamping the real story of Sub Pop Rock City as completely as the punk postcards dampened down the Spirit of '77 in London.

Truth was that by the summer of 1992, Sub Pop Rock City was dead. The underground had triumphed or been betrayed, depending where you stood. Pavitt and Poneman's label still functioned, soaking up the welcome royalties from Nirvana albums, but having lost all of the bands who created the Sub Pop sound. And the indie alternative was no longer alternative, or independent. Nirvana were at DGC; Pearl Jam, Screaming Trees and Alice In Chains at Sony; Soundgarden on A&M; Mudhoney at Warners; Tad was discussing a deal with RCA; even The Melvins, the instigators of the local grunge scene, were signing with Atlantic, via a contract insisting that Kurt Cobain produce their first album.

The true Seattle underground had moved twenty or thirty miles around Puget Sound, to Olympia - home of K Records, Kill Rock Stars, and the fervent champions of Riot Grrrl rock. Back in Seattle, the town was filling with another wave of immigrants - musicians, this time, mostly from the evil empire of Seattle's sworn enemy, California, travelling north to meet the expectations of the lame and late A&R men who descended upon the local rock scene throughout 1992 in search of the new Nirvana. There was a delicious irony in California chequebooks being waved at Californians simply because they'd moved north a few

months earlier: small wonder that Mudhoney, in the most intelligent song on the *Singles* soundtrack, declared their hometown 'Overblown'.

Seattle rock is dead, then: the city's musicians have become the world's. By the end of 1993, the mere mention of Seattle will be enough to quash a new band's prospects. Locals will be forced to migrate to California, or else build another underground, ripe for the picking early in the 21st century.

Meanwhile, for Pearl Jam, Soundgarden and the rest, major-label life will continue. For Nirvana, though, the future is less certain. They ended 1992 as most magazines' band of the year - a year when they issued nothing but singles from 'Nevermind', and then a compilation, neatly titled 'Incesticide', which rounded up stray B-sides, giveaways, demos and Sub Pop rarities. Kurt Cobain penned some typically vitriolic notes for the record, which DGC had to omit when their lawyers began to talk about the concept of libel.

Choosing their outlets carefully, Cobain and Courtney Love continued to give sporadic interviews to those known to be sympathetic to their cause. Prime among them was *The Advocate*, America's leading gay/lesbian magazine. Already chosen by k.d. lang as the venue for her public coming-out, *The Advocate* landed another scoop early in 1993 when it ran a story somewhat spuriously titled 'The Dark Side Of Kurt Cobain'. It revealed the supposedly zombie-like singer as intelligent, literate, self-mocking, and also a willing convert to the gay cause.

It was just like the jocks in the Aberdeen bars had thought: the Cobain kid was a faggot, after all. Well, nearly: "I'm definitely gay in spirit," he conceded, "and I probably could be bisexual. If I wouldn't have found Courtney, I probably would have carried on with a bisexual lifestyle." And he trawled through the past - from the years of antagonising local sexual mores in Aberdeen, to the more recent scars cut by the shiny pages of *Vanity Fair*.

Cobain probably reckoned he'd laid the ghosts of that exposure to rest when he issued a three-page 'open letter' towards the end of 1992. It took the form of a rambling memoir, which began on the streets of West Kensington in London as he searched for the first Raincoats album, then for the former members of the band. He made contact with Raincoats mainstay Ana, and a few days later, after what he'd perceived as a cold encounter, she sent him an autographed copy of the record.

"It was one of the few really important things that I've been blessed with since becoming an untouchable boy genius," Cobain wrote with a touching mixture of affection and irony. And he listed the other moments that had cut through the industry bullshit - recruiting Shonen Knife or

The Vaselines as Nirvana's support bands, "being asked to support Sonic Youth on two tours, totally being taken under their wing and being showed what dignity really means"; on through a series of human contacts among musicians, of unsolicited moments of kindness or faith, "or being a part of one of L7's pro-choice benefits in L.A., or kissing Chris and Dave on *Saturday Night Live* just to spite homophobes, or meeting Iggy Pop..." and on and on.

After a frenzied assault on Lynn Hirschberg and what he saw as "lies", Cobain switched to another set of accusations: those which pegged him as the betrayer of some holy notion of punk rock. "I don't feel the least bit guilty for commercially exploiting a completely exhausted Rock Youth Culture", he wrote, "because at this point in rock history, Punk Rock is, to me, dead and gone." And he ended with another switch of arena - pleading with fans who don't share his tolerance for racial and sexual difference to "leave us the fuck alone - don't come to our shows and don't buy our records". There was nothing left to sell out, he seemed to be saying, except his own principles; and those he would defend to the end.

The next step of the story was supposed to be gentle: fatherhood, a slow return to stability, and then in February 1993 the sessions for the new album. Instead, the ripples of the *Vanity Fair* story continued to slop over the side of the ship. "We are decent, ethical people," Cobain had asserted in his 'open letter'; but the Victoria Clarke/Britt Collins episode threatened to tilt public opinion against him.

Clarke and Collins had begun work on a Nirvana biography early in 1992. Initially, they seem to have been accepted by Cobain and Love, but by the late summer, communications between the band and the prospective authors had broken down. Clarke did manage to interview Chris Novoselic for the project, but the revelation that she'd also spoken to Lynn Hirschberg triggered a violent reaction from the Cobains. In October, first Love and then Cobain left a series of bitter messages on Clarke's ansaphone; in December, Love is alleged to have assaulted Clarke in a Hollywood bar. From there, the layers of disinformation multiplied, each side claiming innocent virtue in the face of rampant egotism and irrationality.

Early in 1993, selections of the ansaphone tapes were published for the first time, in the British rock magazine *Select*. "We will use every dollar we have and every bit of our power to basically fuck you up," Love was quoted as saying. "I don't know why I'm trying to be fucking rational with you, most people want to fucking kill you at this point."

The dialogue attributed to Cobain was starker, less coherent, more confused: "I have a lot of things to say to you, a lot of things... you

SOUNDGARDEN'S 'BADMOTORFINGER' ALBUM FINALLY TRANSPORTED THEIR STADIUM-BOUND HARD ROCK INTO ITS NATURAL ARENA.

parasitic little cunts. If you... if *anything* comes out in this book which hurts my wife, I'll fucking hurt *you*. I'm at the end of my ropes... I've never been more serious in my life... I suppose I could throw out a few thousand dollars to have you snuffed out, but maybe I'll try it the legal way first... What does it feel like to fuck your way through interviews?"

Suddenly, decency, ethics and sexism were concepts that needed redefining.

Until Cobain, Grohl and Novoselic arrived for sessions at Steve Albini's studio in February 1993, it was hard to remember that Nirvana had once been a band. They cut an album's worth of basic tracks in three days, then paused while Cobain searched through eighteen months of extreme experiences for lyrical inspiration. The word was out in advance: this was not another *Nevermind*, but a deliberate puncturing of the band's pop godhead. Cobain wanted to abdicate from a crown that was garnished with golden thorns.

Outside, the world of high fashion - not deserving the tag 'the real world' - had decided that grunge was chic. Designers turned into fools and created $500 lookalikes of $10 sweaters; the real fools were those who took the entire 'creation' seriously enough to be offended. All the episode proved was that the chasm between innovation and acceptance was fast becoming invisible. In less than a year, Seattle had moved from mecca to cliché: once the catwalks were on the case, the smell of rotting culture couldn't be far behind.

With Pearl Jam, Soundgarden, Screaming Trees and the rest translated from Washington State into a stadium large enough to encompass the globe, the sound of Seattle was nothing more than a memory. Nirvana belonged just as much to the world, though they preferred death by elitism to death by numbers. Presented with a stark choice between stardom and self-destruction, they seemed to have elected for a deliciously violent ending.

Exactly how violent, though, was still open to debate. Steve Albini leaked acidic droplets of misinformation, all helping to construct the myth of a gloriously perverse record, a deliberate cleansing of the past. The press picked up song titles - not just the expected 'Rape Me' and 'Dumb', which had been in the band's live set for months, but 'Serve The Servants' and 'Frances Farmer', with which Cobain would be reclaiming the right to create his own legend. Nirvana's left-field credibility was duly enhanced. Within a few weeks, though, the band were back in the public arena, arguing over the definition of truth via press releases. It was the *Vanity Fair* debacle replayed: while that magazine had seemed to be twisting a knife between Cobain and Courtney Love, the *Chicago Tribune* and then *Newsweek* in May were forcing a chasm between the band and their beloved label. In the *Tribune*, Albini was quoted as saying that Geffen wouldn't want to issue the record - titled, at least in theory, 'I Hate Myself And I Want To Die'. Later, the title was changed to 'In Utero'. "I have no faith this record will be released," Albini crowed. "It's not a record for wimps." Heaven forbid.

Enter Jeff Giles of *Newsweek*, who upped the ante by declaring (in a piece wittily headed "You Call This Nirvana?") that Geffen regarded the Nirvana album as "unreleasable", and quoting Albini's verdict on the saga: "a fracas". Not for the first time, Nirvana resorted to a press release, and a letter to the news magazine reprinted as a paid advertisement in the hallowed pages of the trade mag, *Billboard*. "Jeff Giles has written an article on our band which was not based on the band's views nor on information provided by our representatives," opened the letter to *Newsweek*, with a blatant disregard for journalistic independence. Giles' crime, it seemed, was to rely on "unnamed sources and 'music industry insiders'". "Most damaging to us," the band's letter concluded, "is that Giles ridiculed our relationship with our label based on totally erroneous information. Geffen Records has supported our efforts all along in making this record."

In a press release, Cobain went further - confirming that the band had "spent two weeks with Albini recording some of the best tracks we've ever done, and most of the mixes from that session are perfect. However, Steve would not spend much time on the mixes and overall we - the band - felt the vocals were not loud enough on a few of the tracks." And Cobain couldn't resist a sneer at Albini's holier-than-thou attitude to recording: "Steve has made a career out of being anti-rock establishment, but being commercial or anti-commercial is not what makes a good rock record, it's the songs. And until we have the songs recorded the way we want them, Nirvana will not release the record."

By almost confirming rumours of a creative rift between Nirvana and Albini, Kurt Cobain had set out the pitch for a rollerball derby of rumours and counter-rumours. With any other band - the carefully calculating U2, for instance - it might all have been publicity for the record. With Nirvana, there was always the danger that the group's precarious unity and purpose might begin to fracture under pressure.

Trust Courtney Love to capture the mood of the times. While the outside world sweated over the future of Nirvana, Love summed up her private psychodrama in a single record - Hole's 'Beautiful Son', issued in April 1993. "You look good in my dress/my beautiful son", she sang to the pretty teenager on the cover of the single - a deadringer for Kurt Cobain, headed for the womb in preference to a public execution. And so that no-one could miss the point, Courtney backed the song with a tribute to Yoko Ono - once publicly called 'Mother' by her most famous husband. From Sid and Nancy to John and Yoko was a canny shift of emphasis - remember, only one of those four archetypes actually survived. Nirvana may, after all, prove to have been nothing more than a dramatic subplot in a Love story with a difference. Given Cobain's 'liberated' sexual politics, that's maybe as fitting an ending as any.

GRUNGE IS DEAD, BUT THE GRUNGE DYNASTY LIVES ON. FATHER AND DAUGHTER COBAIN REFUTE THE 'DRUG BABY' RUMOURS.

Seattle & sub pop chronology

1979
Bruce Pavitt publishes the first of his *Subterranean Pop* fanzines.

1980
14-year-old Andrew Wood and his brother Kevin form the first line-up of Malfunkshun.

1981
The Melvins play their first gigs in Aberdeen. Kurt Cobain is given his first guitar.
Mark Arm forms Mr Epp & The Calculations, and moonlights in a good-time punk band, The Limp Richards, alongside Ducky Boys guitarist Steve Turner.

1982
Mr Epp and The Calculations issue their only record, an EP entitled 'Of Course I'm Happy. Why?'
Chris Cornell joins Hiro Yamamoto's band, The Shemps; Yamamoto leaves within weeks, and is replaced by Kim Thayil.
Courtney Love spends several months in Liverpool, where she is closely associated with Julian Cope.

1983
The Ducky Boys split up: Steve Turner joins Mark Arm in Mr Epp.
April - Bruce Pavitt's first monthly 'Sub Pop' column appears in Seattle magazine *The Rocket*.

1984
Kurt Cobain is introduced to Chris Novoselic. The pair play their first local gigs in Aberdeen, under such names as Ed, Ted & Fred and Skid Row.
Green River evolves out of Mr Epp and Spluii Numa, recording their first demos in Seattle.
Around the same time, the initial line-up of Soundgarden is assembled out of the remains of The Shemps.
Courtney Love, Kat Bjelland and Jennifer Finch form Sugar Baby Doll in Portland.
December - Green River record their debut EP, 'Come On Down'.

1985
Summer - Andrew Wood's parents commit him to Cabrini Hospital in an attempt to break his heroin addiction.
Kurt Cobain is arrested on vandalism charges in Aberdeen.
Autumn - C/Z Records issue the 'Deep Six' compilation LP, featuring tracks by Malfunkshun, Green River, Soundgarden, The Melvins, The U-Men and Skin Yard.
Courtney Love is among the cast for Alex Cox's movie *Straight To Hell*, being filmed on location in Spain.

1986
Matt Cameron joins Soundgarden.
February 8 - The Melvins record their début album with Jack Endino in Seattle.
June - Green River record their 'Dry As A Bone' EP.
July - Sub Pop issue the 'Sub Pop 100' compilation.
September - In Aberdeen, Kurt Cobain records the first Nirvana demo tape with Melvins drummer Dale Crover.

1987
Jerry Cantrell and Layne Staley form their first band, the Fucks.
Spring - Nirvana, now Cobain, Novoselic and Crover, record another demo tape, this time with Jack Endino in Seattle.
June - Sub Pop issue Green River's 'Dry As A Bone' and Soundgarden's 'Hunted Down'.
August - Green River begin work on their 'Rehab Doll' album.
October - After a dispute over ethics, Green River split up.

1988
The Fucks become Alice 'N Chains (subsequently Alice In Chains).
Spring - Nirvana record their debut single, 'Love Buzz'.
March - Mother Love Bone, who include ex-members of Green River and Malfunkshun, hold their first rehearsals.
June - Mother Love Bone record their first set of professional demos. Geffen show an immediate interest in signing the band.
July - Bruce Pavitt writes his final 'Sub Pop' column for *The Rocket*.
August - An article in the *Tacoma News Tribune* cites Soundgarden, Young Fresh Fellows, the Dan Reed Network and Uncle Bonsai as prime movers in an influx of North-Western talent.
Mudhoney release their debut single on Sub Pop, 'Touch Me I'm Sick'/'Sweet Young Thing Ain't Sweet No More'.
October - Mudhoney release their 'Superfuzz Bigmuff' mini-LP.
Nirvana issue their debut single, 'Love Buzz'/'Big Cheese'.
November - Sub Pop issue 'Sub Pop 200' as a 3-LP edition of 5,000 copies.
Soundgarden issue their SST album, 'Ultramega OK'.
November 19 - Mother Love Bone sign with Mercury/Polygram.
December - Soundgarden begin recording their major label debut, 'Louder Than Love'.
Tinnitus Records issues the 'Away From The Pulsebeat Presents Mondostereo' LP, featuring Mudhoney's 'Hate The Police'.

1989
Music by Mother Love Bone and Soundgarden is included on the soundtrack of Cameron Crowe's movie, *Say Anything*.
January - The Sub Pop single combining Mudhoney's 'Halloween' and Sonic Youth's 'Touch Me I'm Sick' is released.
February - Over the next month, around 20 Seattle bands make a concentrated assault on the San Francisco market, including Skin Yard, Coffin Break, Hester Prynne, The Melvins, Blood Circus, Soundgarden, Mudhoney and Nirvana, who support The Melvins at the CW Saloon.
Glitterhouse reissue Green River's 'Rehab Doll' EP — the first release by the band in Europe — and Mudhoney's 'Superfuzz Bigmuff'.
March -*Rolling Stone* profiles Soundgarden: "They're young, talented and too cool to stay in school."
Mercury issue Mother Love Bone's debut EP, 'Shine'.
Sonic Youth and Mudhoney tour the U.K.*M*
March 11 - To the amazement of Seattle journalists, Everett True's feature on Mudhoney is chosen as *Melody Maker*'s cover story.
April -Jason Everman joins Nirvana as second guitarist.
Sub Pop release Tad's album, 'God's Balls'.
May - Release date for Mudhoney's 'You Got It'/'Burn It Clean' single.
Soundgarden tour the UK, to coincide with the release of their SST single, 'Flower'.
May 4 - Mother Love Bone play a homecoming show at the Oz Nightclub to celebrate the end of their first national tour. Their support act is Alice In Chains.
May 10 - Mudhoney begin their first U.K. headlining tour at the Norwich Arts Centre, supported in London by Soundgarden. During their visit, they also record their first session for John Peel's Radio 1 show.
June -Sub Pop present Lamefest '89 at the Moore Theatre in Seattle, showcasing Mudhoney, Tad and Nirvana.
Sub Pop release Nirvana's début album, 'Bleach'. The group record 'Been A Son' and 'Stain' with Steve Fisk, rather than Jack Endino, as producer.
Island Records begin a series of meetings with Bruce Pavitt and Jonathan Poneman to discuss a distribution deal for Sub Pop.
July - Nirvana appear at a New Music Seminar concert at Maxwell's in Hoboken, across the river from Manhattan, sharing a bill in the 200-capacity club with Mudhoney. Shortly after the show, Everman quits the band to join Soundgarden.
August - Mother Love Bone begin sessions for their debut album at the Plant, Sausalito.
August 12 - Nirvana's 'Bleach' LP is issued in

the U.K. by Tupelo.

August 25/26 - Sub Pop present two nights of music and video at the Seattle Center of Contemporary Art.

September - Alice In Chains send a "shitty eight-track" demo tape to Columbia Records.

October - Southern and Glitterhouse issue the eponymous debut full-length LP by Mudhoney. Soundgarden bassist Hiro Yamamoto quits the band as their 'Louder Than Love' album is released. Jason Everman joins for a U.S. tour. Mudhoney release the 'This Gift'/'Baby Help Me Forget' single.

Amphetamine Reptile Records issue their 'Dope, Guns & Fucking In The Street' compilation, featuring tracks by the Thrown Ups.

October 23 - Tad and Nirvana open a British tour at the Newcastle Riverside, supported by Scottish band the Cateran. Tupelo issue Nirvana's 'Blew' 12" EP to coincide with the concerts.

October 26 - Nirvana cancel a Reading show to record their first John Peel session.

November - Nirvana and Tad play shows in Berlin during the collapse of the Berlin Wall. When they return to Seattle, Tad begin recording sessions with producer Butch Vig.

November 20 - Andrew Wood begins detox treatment for heroin addiction at the Valley General Hospital Drug/Alcohol Recovery Center in Monroe.

November - Mudhoney begin another U.K. tour.

December - Jason Everman is sacked from Soundgarden. "He just didn't work out," says guitarist Kim Thayil.

Mudhoney, Nirvana and Tad stage a U.K. version of the Lamefest 89 show at the Astoria in London.

Tad release their 'Wood Goblins' 12" single on Sub Pop.

A Mudhoney bootleg single, combining live versions of 'You Got It' and 'In 'N' Out Of Grace', begins to circulate, under the title Grunge-R-Us.

December 15 - A survey of U.S. college radio programmers by *Rockpool* magazine quotes Mudhoney as their most-preferred band.

1990

January - Nirvana are reported to have almost completed their second Sub Pop album. They tour California and Washington with Tad.

February - Columbia agree to sign Alice In Chains.

A riot interrupts a Melvins show in Tacoma, after the promoter cuts the power when members of the audience refuse to stop stagediving. The Melvins play a barrage of Kiss covers until the promoter relents.

The Mudhoney compilation LP 'Boiled Beef And Rotting Teeth' is released.

Nirvana support Screaming Trees and Tad at several North-West shows.

February 21 - Soundgarden are nominated for, but fail to win, a Grammy in the Best Hard Rock Album category.

March - Tupelo issue a single combining the Melvins' cover of Mudhoney's 'Sweet Young Thing Ain't Sweet No More' and Steelpole Bathtub's version of 'I Dreamed I Dream', in artwork parodying the 1988 Mudhoney/Sonic Youth joint single.

Tad's 'Salt Lick' album, produced by Steve Albini, is released by Sub Pop.

A&M distribute a Soundgarden promo CD, 'Louder Than Live!'.

More Nirvana sessions are scheduled, with Butch Vig as producer.

Sub Pop begin negotiations with CBS/Sony over a major-label distribution deal.

March 16 - Andrew Wood is found unconscious at his Queen Anne apartment by his girlfriend, Xanna LaFuente.

March 19 - Doctors at Harborview Medical Center shut down Andrew Wood's life support systems, after tests showed he was not going to recover from his coma.

March - A memorial tribute to Andrew Wood is held at the Paramount Theatre in Seattle.

March 27 - The King County Medical Examiner's Division confirms that Andrew Wood's death was due to "accidental and acute overdose of opiates".

April - Mother Love Bone's LP 'Apple' is issued.

Tupelo's Singles Club is launched with Dickless's cover of Rare Earth's 'I'm A Man'. Unissued Soundgarden material is included on SST's compilation album, 'Programme Annhilator II'. The band tour Britain, promoting their 'Hands All Over' EP, but their subsequent visit to Italy is aborted when Matt Cameron contracts acute food poisoning.

Babes In Toyland's debut LP, 'Spanking Machine', is released by Twin Tone.

May - Nirvana play a lengthy series of club shows down the East Coast of America. The band now plan to have their second LP ready "by the fall".

'The Winding Sheet', the début solo LP by Mark Lanegan of the Screaming Trees, is released, featuring instrumental support from Nirvana's Kurt Cobain and Chris Novoselic.

The U.S. compilation 'Crunchouse' is released, featuring contributions from Mudhoney, Tad and the Thrown Ups.

June - Chad Channing leaves Nirvana. The band are still reported to be about to record their second album.

The first Alice In Chains record, an EP entitled 'We Die Young', is released by Columbia. Tad tour Britain.

Jeff Ament and Stone Gossard begin tentative rehearsals for their first post-Mother Love Bone band.

June 18 - Waterfront issue the Sub Pop compilation, 'Fuck Me I'm Rich'.

June 19-21 - Mudhoney play three nights at the Hibernian on London's Fulham Broadway.

July - J. Mascis of Dinosaur Jr is rumoured to have auditioned with Nirvana as replacement drummer for Chad Channing.

Mudhoney issue their 'Thorn' EP, while the first Mudhoney bootleg LP appears - 'Live In Hollywood'.

Soundgarden made a return visit to Britain, promoting their A&M single 'Loud Love'.

Hole's debut single, 'Retard Girl', is issued on Sympathy For The Record Industry.

Dan Peters of Mudhoney is the latest name linked to the vacant role of drummer in Nirvana.

July 30 - Waterfront Records issue a collection of Kiss covers called 'Hard To Believe', including Nirvana's 'Do You Love Me'.

August - Nirvana continue work on a second album for Sub Pop with producer Butch Vig. Six tracks are completed.

Green River's 'Dry As A Bone' finally receives its UK debut release on Tupelo.

Mudhoney perform at the Reading Festival, after headlining a show at the Motorsports International Garage in Seattle with Thee Headcoats and Beat Happening in support.

September - Alice In Chains' debut LP, 'Facelift', is issued on Columbia.

Tad drummer Steve Wied quits the band. Nirvana support Sonic Youth at a Seattle show. The Thrown-Ups issue their eponymous debut album on Amphetamine Reptile.

Sub Pop reissue Soundgarden's early EPs, 'Screaming Life' and 'Fopp', as a CD.

Soundgarden take part in the Cult's Gathering Of The Tribes festival at the Pacific Amphitheatre in Los Angeles, on a bill which also includes the Charlatans, the Quireboys, the Mission and Iggy Pop.

Proposed release date for a Nirvana single on Sub Pop called 'Rag Burn'.

Eddie Vedder arrives in Seattle to join Jeff Ament and Stone Gossard's new band, quickly named Mookie Blaylock.

October - Nirvana headline a four-band bill at the Motorsports International Garage in Seattle, supported by the Melvins, the Dwarves and the Derelicts. After this show, Dan Peters is dropped from the band, deemed "not heavy enough" by Kurt Cobain. His replacement is Dave Grohl from Washington DC hardcore band Scream.

October 23 - Nirvana begin a U.K. tour (supported by L7). Sub Pop schedule their 'Sliver' single to coincide with the tour, but the release is cancelled until December 1 to allow the label to build up sufficient stock of the single to satisfy advance retail orders. During the tour, the band record a second session for John Peel, covering songs by Devo, The Wipers and The Vaselines.

November - Work begins on the 'Temple Of The Dog' tribute album to Andrew Wood.

Mudhoney's Mark Arm issues a solo single on Sub Pop - a cover of Bob Dylan's 'Masters Of War'.

Glitterhouse release the singles boxed set 'Endangered Species', featuring Green River's 'Ain't Nothin' To Do'.

Negotiations over a distribution deal between CBS and Sub Pop break down.

After completing their U.K. tour, Nirvana play several West Coast shows with the Melvins and Dickless.

November 3 - Imaginary Records issue 'Heaven And Hell: A Tribute To The Velvet Underground', which includes Nirvana's cover of 'Here She Comes Now'.

December - Nirvana are officially reported as being "at loggerheads" with Sub Pop, though still planning to issue their second album through the label in the spring.

1991

January - Tad's 'Jack Pepsi' single is issued by Sub Pop, drawing complaints from the Pepsi-Cola organisation.

Nirvana begin pre-production work on their next album.

January 4 - It is revealed that Nirvana have signed a two-album contract with Geffen Records.

February - Sub Pop issue Mudhoney's compilation EP 'Hate The Police', and Tad's '8-Way Santa' LP.

February 25 - Rehearsals begin in Seattle for Cameron Crowe's movie *Singles*.

March - Soundgarden begin work on 'Badmotorfinger'.

March/April - Butch Vig supervises recording sessions for Nirvana's 'Nevermind' at Sound City, Van Nuys, California.

Nirvana play their first North-West show since signing with Geffen, supporting Screaming Trees at the Commodore Ballroom in Vancouver.

March - *Singles* begins shooting in Seattle.

April - Hole's 'Dicknail' single is issued by Sub Pop.

'Temple Of The Dog' is released.

Amphetamine Reptile issue their *Ugly American Overkill* compilation, featuring the Thrown-Ups' 'Stockboy Superhero'.

April 11 - Sonic Youth visit the set of *Singles*, escorted by Mudhoney's Mark Arm.

April 22 - Jeff Ament of Mookie Blaylock delivers a rehearsal tape of the band's proposed songs for the *Singles* soundtrack.

April 28 - Alice In Chains' show at Desoto is filmed for *Singles*.

May 24 - Initial shooting on *Singles* is completed.

June - Kurt Cobain and Courtney Love are spotted together in Los Angeles at a Butthole Surfers show.

July 22 - Sub Pop issue Mudhoney's 'Let It Slide' single.

August 20-25 - The International Pop Underground Convention is staged in Olympia. Besides a Sub Pop barbeque, there are shows by Beat Happening, the Melvins, Jad Fair, the Pastels, Thee Headcoats, Fugazi and L7.

August 5 - Hole preview their debut album with the 'Teenage Whore' single.

August 12 - Mudhoney's final album for Sub Pop, 'Every Good Boy Deserves Fudge', is released. On the same day, the band begin a U.K. tour at the London Astoria, supported by Hole.

Nirvana play the Reading Festival, having warmed up with shows in Ireland.

September - DGC supply MTV with the video for Nirvana's 'Smells Like Teen Spirit', which wins a place in the station's 'Buzz Bin' slot.

Alice In Chains' 'Facelift' achieves gold record status - the first such award for a Seattle 'alternative' band.

Soundgarden are invited to support Guns 'N Roses on a US tour, scheduled for October but eventually postponed until December.

Communion records pair two of the tracks from Imaginary's album of Velvet Underground covers as a single - Nirvana's 'Here She Comes Now' and The Melvins' 'Venus In Furs'.

September 17 - Hole's 'Pretty On The Inside' is issued in the States.

September 24 - DGC issue just 50,000 copies of Nirvana's 'Nevermind' LP in the States. The album is also issued in Britain, on the same day as Hole's 'Pretty On The Inside'.

October - Nirvana finally make the cover of Seattle's rock paper, *The Rocket*.

Soundgarden support Metallica at the Day On The Green show in Oakland.

October 8 - Soundgarden's *Badmotorfinger* LP is released after delays over the cover art.

October - Nirvana share the bill with Smashing Pumpkins at several East Coast U.S. shows. Police question the band after a Washington DC hotel room is trashed.

October 23 - The *Seattle Weekly* runs an exposé asking: "Is Sub Pop about to pop?"

October 31 - Soundgarden appear at the Day On The Green festival in Oakland, supporting Metallica and Faith No More.

Nirvana are supported by Mudhoney in a surprise show at the Paramount Theatre in Seattle.

November - Alice In Chains are voted Best New Band of 1991 by the readers of *Guitar*.

Pearl Jam play their first New York show, at CBGBs.

Nirvana tour Britain (playing shows in Bristol, London and Wolverhampton) and Europe, where their Amsterdam Paradiso show is filmed for Dutch TV — part of a programme in which there are also interviews with Dave Grohl and Chris Novoselic, and Geffen Records staff.

Another TV appearance is on *The Word*, where Kurt Cobain happily describes Courtney Love as "the greatest fuck in the world". They also

record a session for BBC Radio 1's Mark Goodier show.

Hole tour Britain, and record a session for the John Peel show.

Back in California, Nirvana and Hole play the Palace Theatre in Los Angeles, watched by Axl Rose and Perry Farrell.

Representatives from Madonna's management company, DeMann Entertainments, contact Hole's lawyer Rosemary Carol to discuss the band signing to Madonna's new record label, Maverick.

November - The first preview screening of *Singles* is held in Seattle.

November 16 - 'Nevermind' reaches the *Billboard* Top 10.

November 18 - Geffen issue 'Smells Like Teen Spirit' in Britain.

December - Soundgarden tour the U.S. with Guns 'N Roses.

Nirvana are named as possible headliners for the second Lollapalooza tour. In Rennes, France, they play their final European concert before cancelling the remainder of their tour, including two Irish shows, when Kurt Cobain loses his voice.

December 10 - Hole begin another short series of U.K. shows.

December - Courtney Love makes her first public response to Madonna's interest in Hole: "The world's not big enough for her to be my boss, but I'll go out to dinner with her if she pays!"

December 21 - Pearl Jam are special guests at an Alice In Chains show at the Paramount Theatre, Seattle.

December 24-31 - 'Nevermind' sells 373,520 copies in the final week of 1991. During December 1991, Bleach also sells 70,000 copies.

December - Nirvana and Pearl Jam support the Red Hot Chili Peppers at a New Year's Eve show at the Cow Palace in San Francisco.

1992

January - On consecutive nights, Nirvana perform live on MTV and *Saturday Night Live* — culminating their appearance on the latter when Kurt and Chris indulge in a sloppy French kiss. The 'offending' sequence is duly cut when the show is repeated later in the year.

Nirvana tour Australia, New Zealand, Japan and Hawaii, in a eries of concerts carrying through to February. To coincide with the Japanese shows, Geffen issue a Japan-only CD, 'Hormoaning', which includes material from the band's second John Peel show, plus two B-sides.

Nirvana's early appearance on a 'Teriyaki Asthma' EP, performing 'Mexican Seafood', is included on a compilation CD of the first five releases in the series, on C/Z.

The Washington State band Courtney Love are advised that they can no longer use that name: they split up shortly afterwards.

Nirvana's 'Beeswax' is included on the K Records compilation, 'Kill Rock Stars', issued to celebrate the 1991 International Pop Underground festival in Olympia.

January 1 - Chris Cornell of Soundgarden delivers a collection of incidental music pieces for consideration on the *Singles* soundtrack.

January 3 - Pearl Jam open for Red Hot Chili Peppers at the Seattle Center Arena.

January 21 - DGC issue 'Come As You Are', the second single from 'Nevermind'.

January 24 - Warner Brothers suggest that Cameron Crowe change the title of his movie from *Singles* to *Come As You Are*.
Sales of 'Nevermind' top three million.

January 29 - 'Nevermind' returns to the top of the *Billboard* Albums Chart.

January - Courtney Love and Sonic Youth's Kim Gordon co-host a cable chat show - Kurt Cobain having turned the offer down.

February - Alice In Chains issue their 'Sap' EP. Soundgarden begin a U.S. tour, supporting Skid Row.
Pearl Jam play what is effectively a guests-only show at the Borderline in London. To appease disappointed fans outside the venue, members of the band distribute free promo CDs to those in the queue.

February 10 - Nirvana deny rumours that they will be appearing at the 1992 Reading Festival.

February 17 - Pearl Jam's 'Alive' is issued in Britain.

February 24 - Kurt Cobain and Courtney Love are married in Waikiki, Hawaii by a female non-denominational minister, with a roadie as witness.
Pearl Jam's debut LP, 'Ten', appears in Britain.

February 28 - Bassist Jill Emery quits Hole after a show at the Whisky A Go Go in Los Angeles.

March - While in Los Angeles to play a Rock The Vote concert, Mudhoney sign a recording deal with Warner Brothers.

March 2 - Nirvana's second single from *Nevermind*, 'Come As You Are', is released.

March 4/6 - Soundgarden and the Melvins play the Paramount Theatre in Seattle.

March - Soundgarden begin a UK tour.
Kurt Cobain is reported to be assembling a fanzine devoted to attacking prejudice on grounds of race, gender or sexual orientation.

March 23 - *Time* magazine recognises "The Puget Sound is the hottest in rock".

March 30 - Soundgarden issue their 'Jesus Christ Pose' single. MTV restrict screenings of their video for the song, alleging it will offend religious minds.

April - Mudhoney head the bill at Sub Pop's Ultra Lamefest at Seattle's Paramount Theatre. Kurt and Courtney appear as cover stars in the American subversive teen mag, *Sassy*. The couple buy a new woodland home outside Seattle.
Nirvana record 'Oh The Guilt' in a basement studio in Washington DC, specifically for a joint single with The Jesus Lizard first mooted in 1989.
Hole record 'Beautiful Friend' and 'Doll Parts' for a forthcoming single. Courtney Love announces that she is pregnant, and that her child will be called either Frances B. Kobain or Coal B. Kobain.

April 2 - A local religious group mark Soundgarden's performance in Bristol with demonstrations as a protest against their 'Jesus Christ Pose' artwork.

May - Hard Rock Comics publish *Nirvana*, a laughable comic-strip history of the band's rise to fame.
Nirvana begin a U.S. tour.
Hole replace drummer Caroline with ex-Dumbhead stickswoman Patti.

May - The City of Seattle Parks Department withdraws permission for Pearl Jam's 18 May free show at Gas Works Park, supported by Seaweed.

June - Nirvana reveal plans to issue a joint single with The Jesus Lizard, on the Touch & Go label.
Rumours spread that Kurt Cobain has been killed in a car accident, but he survives long enough to play Irish dates with Nirvana.

June 6 - Soundgarden take part in a French pay-for-view TV special with Guns 'N Roses and Faith No More. Their 'Badmotorfinger' LP is repackaged with a bonus EP in readiness for the Lollapalooza tour.
Pearl Jam perform at the Cult's day-long festival in London's Finsbury Park.

June 27 - Sub Pop win the Joel Webber Award for excellence in music and business at the New Music Seminar in New York, drawing ironic smiles from those employees affected in recent months by the label's financial problems.

June - Kurt Cobain collapses with a "mystery virus" after a show at Balfast King's Hall.
Pearl Jam are forced to cancel two London shows after vocalist Eddie Vedder collapses with exhaustion.

July - Kurt Cobain returns from Nirvana's European tour to find that his Seattle apartment has been flooded, destroying several books of lyrics and poetry he'd been storing in the shower.
The Lollapalooza II tour opens, featuring Soundgarden and Pearl Jam. The night before the tour begins, Temple Of The Dog play an unscheduled show in Bremerton, Washington.
Cell become the latest 'alternative' signing to DGC, under the label's A&R deal with Sonic Youth's Thurston Moore.
Sub Pop issue the ironically titled 'Revolution Come And Gone' compilation CD, featuring tracks by artists like Hole, Mudhoney, Mark Lanegan and The Walkabouts.
Mudhoney begin work on their first major-label album, at Egg Studios.
Chris Novoselic of Nirvana joins forces with other Seattle campaigners to protest new pro-censorship laws which went into force in Washington State on June 11.
New York band the Action Swingers include a song called 'Courtney Love' on their 'More Fast Numbers' EP.

July 13 - The *Singles* film soundtrack is issued in Britain - six months ahead of the movie.

July - Rumours spread that Kurt Cobain is about to quit Nirvana for a solo career, and that their forthcoming Reading Festival show will be their last.

July 20 - 'Lithium' is released as the third single from the 'Nevermind' album.

August - Nirvana begin to work on material for their forthcoming album.
Rock satirist Weird Al Yankovic issues a spoof single, 'Smells Like Nirvana'.
Killing Joke file a lawsuit in Los Angeles, claiming that Nirvana's 'Come As You Are' has been plagiarised from their 1985 recording, 'Eighties'. In further legal developments, the UK Sixties band called Nirvana fail in their bid to ban Cobain and Co. from 'stealing' their name. Arguments that the Americans' success has harmed their career are dismissed as laughable.
Tim Kerr Records release a singles box set entitled 'Eight Songs For Greg Sage And The Wipers', which includes Nirvana's cover of 'Return Of The Rat' and Hole's version of 'Over The Edge'.
Geffen reissue 'Bleach', complete with two bonus tracks, 'Big Cheese' and 'Downer'.

August 5 - *Vanity Fair* magazine distributes a press release about its forthcoming September issue, headlined: "Rocker Courtney Love is a 'charismatic opportunist' and proud of it".

August 9 - Soundgarden incorporate Ice-T's controversial 'Cop Killer' into their Lollapalooza set.

August 10 - Kurt Cobain and Courtney Love issue a press statement in response to the *Vanity Fair* portrayal of Love.

August 11 - The September issue of *Vanity Fair* reaches the newsstands.

August 17 - Nirvana cancel a 23 August show at the Seattle Center Coliseum because of Courtney Love's advanced state of pregnancy, and Kurt Cobain's hospitalisation with stomach problems.

August 19 - Frances Bean Cobain is born at a Los Angeles hospital.

August 27 - *The Sun* newspaper prints a story alleging that Frances Bean Cobain was born a drug addict.

August 28-30 - Nirvana, L7, Mudhoney and The Melvins all perform at the Reading Festival. In response to mud-throwing, one of L7 removes her tampon and throws it into the audience.
L7 release their 'Monster' single to coincide with the festival.

September - The U.S. scandal-sheet the *Globe* runs a Cobain/Love exposé entitled

"Rock Star's Baby Is Born A Junkie". Nirvana's Chris Novoselic flies to war-torn Croatia, to visit his family.

A&M reissue 'Temple Of The Dog' to capitalise on Pearl Jam's success.

September 9 - Nirvana play live at the MTV Video Music Awards. Backstage, Kurt Cobain and Courtney Love are threatened by Guns 'N Roses vocalist Axl Rose. Nirvana are banned by MTV officials from performing a new song, 'Rape Me', but still collect two awards, 'Smells Like Teen Spirit' winning Best Alternative Video and the band being voted Best New Artists In A Video.

September 11 - Nirvana headline their delayed show in Seattle.

Nirvana headline a concert on behalf of the anti-censorship group, the Washington State Music Coalition.

September 13 - Soundgarden's Chris Cornell and Matt Cameron join Pearl Jam at the end of their Lollapalooza set, to recreate the Temple Of The Dog band. The album has now sold one million copies in America.

September 18 - *Singles* goes on release in the States.

September - Kurt Cobain tells journalist Robert Hilburn about his anti-drug stance, and his continual problems with illness over the last two years.

September 22 - Mercury issue 'Mother Love Bone', a double-CD compilation of the band's entire output.

October - Nirvana record demos for their third album with producer Jack Endino.

Nirvana support Mudhoney in secret shows at the Crocodile Cafe in Seattle and the gymnasium at Bellingham's Western Washington Univ. campus.

October 5 - Mudhoney's major label début, 'Piece Of Cake' on Reprise, is released, coinciding with a UK tour.

October 6 - Julian Cope takes press adverts to promote his 'Fear Loves This Place' EP. The ads are dominated by a Pagan Prayer To The Goddess, with a verse taken to refer to Courtney Love: "Free us (the rock'n'roll fans) from Nancy Spungen fixated heroin a-holes who cling to our greatest rockgroups & suck out their brains..."

November - Alice In Chains' second Columbia album, *Dirt*, is released in Britain.

Steve Albini denies repeated reports in the U.K. press that he has been asked to produce the forthcoming Nirvana album.

Nirvana ask fans to ignore a forthcoming biography, written by Britt Collins and Victoria Clarke - and beg friends to "respect their privacy and decline any requests for interviews".

Stone Gossard completes work on his first 'solo' project since joining Pearl Jam.

November 3 - Soundgarden's home-video *Motorvision* is released.

November 9 - City Slang's double compilation album, 'Tannis Root Presents: Freedom Of Choice - Yesterday's New Wave Hits As Performed By Today's Stars', is released - including Mudhoney's interpretation of Elvis Costello's 'Pump It Up'. Proceeds from the album go to the Planned Parenthood Federation of America.

November 20 - *Vogue* magazine splashes 'grunge fashion' in its December issue.

December - To counter the recent spate of scare stories about their relationship and drug use, Cobain and Love feature in a cover story in *Spin* magazine, interviewed by Sub Pop Records co-founder Jonathan Poneman.

December 1 - The U.S. magazine *Entertainment Weekly* runs a cover story containing a verbal attack by Courtney Love against Nirvana's unofficial biographers. Love later claims that her conversation with journalist Tim Appelo was taped without her knowledge.

December 15 - Nirvana issue a rarities collection, 'Incesticide'. Kurt Cobain's sleeve-notes are omitted from the finished package for legal reasons.

December 19 - *Melody Maker* announce the forthcoming release of 'Let Them Eat Grunge', a mail-order only compilation cassette/CD featuring exclusive tracks by Nirvana, Mudhney, Pond, Seaweed and Afghan Whigs.

December - Steve Albini confirms that he will be producing Nirvana's third album.

December 31 - Pearl Jam support Keith Richards at the Academy, New York.

1993

January - Soundgarden commence work on a new studio album.

Nirvana, L7, Red Hot Chili Peppers and Alice In Chains all perform at the Hollywood Rock Festival in Brazil.

January 11 - Alice In Chains' debut U.K. single, 'Would?', is released. The band's management reveal that Mike Starr is planning to leave the band "because of stress" after completing a forthcoming tour of Europe and their festival appearance in Brazil.

January - Courtney Love announces that she is suing Cedars-Sinai Medical Centre in Los Angeles for illegally giving her medical records to the press.

January 18 - Scheduled release date for Hole's 'Beautiful Son' single, though the record is eventually delayed until April.

January 27 - Alice In Chains and Screaming Trees begin a UK tour.

January 29 - Nirvana's joint single with the Jesus Lizard, 'Oh The Guilt'/'Puss', is issued on Touch & Go.

February - Another major label signing: Tad ink a deal with RCA.

The Nirvana/Sonic Youth concert video, *1991: The Year Punk Broke*, belatedly reaches the shops.

Pearl Jam postpone pre-production work on their follow-up to *Ten*, as Sony feel that their debut album has not yet exhausted its commercial potential.

February 14 - Nirvana begin work on their third album, with Steve Albini producing, at Pachyderm Studios in Minnesota. Basic tracks are completed in three days.

February 18 - Tad release their final Sub Pop recording, the 'Salem' EP.

February - Pearl Jam start rehearsals for their second album.

March - An extended cut of *Singles* is issued by Warner Home Video in the States.

March 2 - Chris Novoselic gives a spoken-word performance at the Royal Festival Hall in London as part of a benefit show for War Child, to raise money for children injured during the conflict in the former Yugoslavia.

March 30 - 'Shame', the début album by Stone Gossard's spin-off band from Pearl Jam, Brad, is released by Columbia.

April 8 - Hole issue their 'Beautiful Son' single — with cover artwork showing a teenage Kurt Cobain.

Nirvana discography

SUB POP SINGLES

Love Buzz/Big Cheese
Sub Pop SP 23 1988 (1,000 copies individually hand-numbered)
Sliver/Dive
Sub Pop SP 72 1990
(3,000 copies on blue vinyl)
Molly's Lips/(Candy by Fluid)
Sub Pop SP 97 1991 (4,000 copies on green vinyl, 3,500 copies on black vinyl)

UK SINGLES

Blew/Love Buzz/Been A Son/Stain
Tupelo TUP EP8 1989 (CD & 12" single)
Sliver/Dive
Tupelo TUP 25 1991
(2,000 copies on green vinyl)
Sliver/Dive/About A Girl
Tupelo TUP EP 25 1991 (12")
Sliver/Dive/About A Girl/Spank Thru
Tupelo TUP CD25 1991 (CD
Smells Like Teen Spirit/Drain You
Geffen DGC5 1991 (also on cassette DGCC 5)
Smells Like Teen Spirit/Even In His Youth/Aneurysm
Geffen DGCT5 1991 (12")
Smells Like Teen Spirit/Even In His Youth/Aneurysm
Geffen DGCT5 1991 (12" picture disc)
Smells Like Teen Spirit/Drain You/Even In His Youth/Aneurysm
Geffen DGCCD5 1991 (CD)
Come As You Are/Endless, Nameless
Geffen DGCT7 1992 (also on cassette DGCC7)
Come As You are/Endless, Nameless/School
Geffen DGCT7 1992 (12")
Come As You are/Endless, Nameless/ School/About A Girl
Geffen DGCTD7 1992 (CD)
Lithium/Curmudgeon
Geffen DGCS9 1992 (also on cassette)
Lithium/Been A Son/Curmudgeon
Geffen DGCTP9 1992 (12")
Lithium/Been A Son/Curmudgeon/D7
Geffen DGCSD9 1992 (CD)
In Bloom/Polly
Geffen GFS 34 1992 (also on cassette)
In Bloom/Sliver (live)/Polly (live)
Geffen GFSTP 34 1992 (12")
In Bloom/Sliver (live)/Polly (live)
Geffen GFSTD 34 1992 (CD
Oh The Guilt/(Puss by The Jesus Lizard)
Toucu & Go TG83 1993 (also on CD TUG 83CD)

ALBUMS

BLEACH
Blew/Floyd The Barber/About A Girl/School/Love Buzz/Paper Cuts/Negative Creeps/Scoffs/Swap Meet/Mr Moustache/Sifting
Tupelo TUP LP6 1989
Originally released as 300 copies on white vinyl, 2,000 on green vinyl.
Subsequently released in 1989 as TUP CD6 with two extra tracks: Love Buzz and Downer.
Subsequently released in 1992 as Geffen GEFD 24433
NEVERMIND
Smells Like Teen Spirit/In Bloom/Come As You Are/Breed/Lithium/Polly/Territorial Pissings/Drain You/Lounge Act/Stay Away/On A Plain/Something Is In the Way
Geffen DGCCD 24425 1991
Released with uncredited bonus track: Endless, Nameless.
INCESTICIDE
Dive/Sliver/Stain/Been A Son/Turn Around/Molly's Lips/Son Of A Gun/(New Wave) Polly/Beeswax/Downer/Mexican Seafood/Hairspray Queen/Aero Zeppelin/Can't be Long Now/Aneurysm
Geffen GED 24504 1992

RELATED RELEASES

SUB POP 200
Sub Pop SP 25 1988
Compilation LP, includes Nirvana's Spank Thru.
HEAVEN AND HELL VOL. 1
Imaginary ILL ILP 016 1990 1990
Compilation LP, includes Nirvana's Here She Comes Now.
TERIYAKI ASTHMA VOL. 1
C/Z 1988
7" compilation, includes Nirvana's Mexican Seafood.
THE WINDING SHEET
Sub Pop SP 61 1990
Mark Lanegan LP, featuring Curt Cobain on two tracks.
HARD TO BELIEVE
Southern 1991
Compilation LP, includes Nirvana's Do You Love Me.
KILL ROCK STARS
K KRS 201 1991
Compilation LP, includes Nirvana's Beeswax
EIGHT SONGS FOR GREG SAGE AND THE WIPERS
C/Z 1992
Singles box set, includes Nirvana's Return Of The Rat and Hole's Over The Edge.

Major releases by related bands

ALICE IN CHAINS

FACELIFT
CBS 467200 2 1990 (LP)
DIRT
CBS 472302 2 1992 (LP)

GREEN RIVER

COME ON DOWN
Homestead HMS 031 1985 (EP)
DEEP SIX
C/Z 1985
Compilation LP, includes track by The Melvins, Soundgarden, Skin Yard, U-Men, Green River & Malfunkshun.
Together We'll Never/Ain't Nothin' To Do
ICP 01 1986 (single)
DRY AS A BONE
Sub Pop SP 11 1987 (EP)
REHAB DOLL
Sub Pop SP 15 1988 (EP)
DRY AS A BONE/REHAB DOLL
Sub Pop SP 11b 1988 (CD)

HOLE

Retard Girl/Phone Bil Song/Johnnie's In the Bathroom
Sympathy For The Record Industry
SFTRI 53 1990 (single)
Dicknail/Burnblack
Sub Pop SP 93 1991 (single)
PRETTY ON THE INSIDE
City Slang SLANG 012 1991 (LP)
SLANGED
City Slang SLANG 25 1992
Compilation LP, includes Hole's Over The Edge
Beautiful Son/20 Years In The Dakota/Old Age
City Sland EFA 04916-03 1993 (single)

MOTHER LOVE BONE

SHINE
Stardog 1989 (EP)
APPLE
Polydor 843 191 2 1990 (LP)
MOTHER LOVE BONE
Polydor 514 177 2 1992 (double CD)

MUDHONEY

Touch Me I'm Sick/Sweet Young Thing Ain't Sweet No More
Sub Pop SP 18 1988 (single)
SUPERFUZZ BIGMUFF
Sub Pop SP 21 1988 (EP)
Halloween/(Touch Me I'm Sick by Sonic Youth)
Sub Pop SP 26 1989 (single)
You Got It/Burn It Clean
Sub Pop SP 33 1989 (single)

KURT HAS PROVIDED THE MUSIC FOR A SINGLE BY NAKED LUNCH AUTHOR WILLIAM BURROUGHS CALLED 'THE PRIEST THEY CALL HIM'.

MUDHONEY
Sub Pop SP 44 1989 (LP)
This Gift/Baby Help me Forget
Sub Pop SP 44AA 1989 (single)
BOILED BEEF & ROTTING TEETH
Sub Pop SP 62 1990 (EP)
Masters Of War/My Life With Rickets
Sub Pop SP 87 1990 (Mark Arm solo single)
EVERY GOOD BOY DESERVES FUDGE
Sub Pop SP 105 1991 (LP)
PIECE OF CAKE
Reprise 9362-45090-2 1992 (LP)

PEARL JAM
TEN
Epic 468884 2 1991 (LP)
SINGLES
Epic 471438 2 1992
Film soundtrack LP, includes tracks by Pearl
Jam, Mudhoney, Paul Westerberg, Mother Love
Bone and Jimi Hendrix.

SOUNDGARDEN
Hunted Down/Nothing To Say
Sub Pop SP 12a 1987 (single)
SCREAMING LIFE
Sub Pop SP 12 1987 (EP)
FOPP
Sub Pop SP 17 1988 (EP)
SCREAMING LIFE/FOPP
Sub Pop 12b 1990 (CD)
ULTRAMEGA OK
SST 201 1988 (LP)
LOUDER THAN LOVE
A&M AMA 5252 1989 (LP)
Room For A Thousand Years Wide/H.I.V. Baby
Sub Pop SP 83 1990 (single)
BADMOTORFINGER
A&M 395 374 2 1991 (LP)

TAD
Ritual Device/Daisy
Sub Pop SP 19 1988 (single)
GOD'S BALLS
Sub Pop SP 27 1989 (LP)
Damaged/(Damaged by Pussy Galore)
Sub Pop SP 37 1989 (single)
SALT LICK
Sub Pop SP 49 1989 (EP)
Loser/Cooking With Glass
Sub Pop SP 55 1990 (single)
8-WAY SANTA
Sub Pop 89 1991 (LP)
SALEM
Sub Pop SPCD 62/229 1992 (EP)

TEMPLE OF THE DOG
TEMPLE OF THE DOG
A&M 393530 2 1991 (LP)